THE

MATT FITZGERALD

COMEBACK QUOTIENT

A GET-REAL GUIDE TO BUILDING MENTAL FITNESS IN SPORT AND LIFE

Boulder, Colorado

5720 Flatiron Parkway
Boulder, CO 80301 USA

VeloPress is the leading publisher of books on endurance sports and is a division of Pocket Outdoor Media. Focused on cycling, triathlon, running, swimming, and nutrition/diet, VeloPress books help athletes achieve their goals of going faster and farther. Preview books and contact us at velopress.com.

Distributed by Ingram Publisher Services

Library of Congress Cataloging-in-Publication Data
Names: Fitzgerald, Matt, author.
Title: The comeback quotient: a get-real guide to building mental fitness in sport and life / Matt Fitzgerald.
Description: Boulder, Colorado: VeloPress, [2020] | Includes bibliographical references and index.
Identifiers: LCCN 2020032189 (print) | LCCN 2020032190 (ebook) | ISBN 9781948007160 (paperback) | ISBN 9781948006262 (ebook)
Subjects: LCSH: Athletes—Psychology. | Sports—Psychological aspects. | Comebacks.
Classification: LCC GV706.4.F52 2020 (print) | LCC GV706.4 (ebook) | DDC 796.01—dc23
LC record available at https://lccn.loc.gov/2020032189
LC ebook record available at https://lccn.loc.gov/2020032190

This paper meets the requirements of ANSI/NISO Z39.48-1992 (Permanence of Paper).

Art direction and interior design by Vicki Hopewell
Cover design by Kevin Roberson
Front cover photo by Kevin Morris
Back cover and p. 213 photo by Tom Hood

20   21   22 / 10   9   8   7   6   5   4   3   2   1

For Cory

Everything that happens is either endurable or not.
If it's endurable, then endure it. Stop complaining.
MARCUS AURELIUS

CONTENTS

PREFACE

On a muggy Thursday evening in September 1993, Rodney Flowers suffered a catastrophic spinal injury while playing JV football for the Pirates of Lumberton, North Carolina. In the blink of an eye, the 15-year-old aspiring pro baller went from star athlete to paraplegic. Doctors told him he would probably never walk again, but today, nearly three decades later, Rodney is not only walking but a successful resilience trainer, author, public speaker, and podcaster—and he credits his mind, above all, for having gotten him from where he was to where he is.

I was nearly done writing this book, with only a short preface left to nail down, when I received an unexpected invitation to be a guest on Rodney's *Game Changer Mentality* podcast. It was also a timely invitation, for the not-quite-finished book I set aside to chat with Rodney was all about comebacks, particularly in the realm of sports, a topic Rodney knows a thing or two about.

Game Changer was more than just an opportunity for me to speak to an expert about a top-of-mind topic. It served also as a helpful reminder that the highest purpose of sport is not to determine winners and losers but rather to train the mind for success—a success that goes well beyond sport. After all, though Rodney did regain the ability to walk, his days as an athlete were over the moment his neck snapped on the gridiron on that fateful late-summer night. Yet it is the athlete inside him that has brought him so far. The same determined mindset that ensured Rodney, rather than any of his teammates, made the flying tackle on the South View Tigers' kick returner that landed him in a wheelchair was what got him out of that wheelchair eventually. "I developed the attitude that whatever it [took] to regain my strength and ability would be exactly what I would dig down and give to the challenge ahead," he writes in his memoir, *Get Up!*

I am hardly alone in believing that the psychology of success in athletics is also the psychology of success in life writ large. Increasingly, psychologists and brain scientists are focusing their research on sport out of a recognition that it has much to teach us about the human mind and behavior. In a 2016 essay titled "Is Sport the Brain's Biggest Challenge?" Vincent Walsh of the Institute of Cognitive Neuroscience at University College London asked, "What makes the best the best? There is an opportunity here to treat . . . elite athletes as case studies from which we can make useful generalizations, much as we have for over a century with neuropsychological single-patient case studies. By studying the abnormal (the elite), we may learn about the population."

The timing of my interview with Rodney was apposite in another way. We spoke at the height of both the COVID-19 pandemic in the US and the social unrest that followed the murder of George Floyd, an unarmed Black man, by a Minneapolis police officer. Eight out of 10 Americans had recently said they believed the country was "out of control" in a nationwide survey. An entire society—indeed, almost the entire world—had been knocked down by the year 2020, and would need to make a comeback of one kind or another.

When I started working on *The Comeback Quotient* in the later part of 2018, I couldn't have imagined what was around the corner. As it turned out, I was affected personally by both of the aforementioned crises, being the husband of an African American woman and coming home from the 2020

Atlanta Marathon infected with virus du jour, which knocked me flat for an entire month. Yet despite the suffering I shared with so many, I couldn't help feeling that, in a small way, these events justified the huge investment of time and energy I'd made in the book while also bringing clarity to the project. In particular, the coronavirus–George Floyd double whammy underscored my belief that setbacks are inescapable in life, hence that all of us need to possess the ability to pull off a comeback.

Some people will come back from 2020 more successfully than others, and a special few will not only survive but thrive, ultimately emerging better than ever, and in so doing they will achieve something that amazes those around them. The most important revelation I had in writing this book was the discovery that, beneath superficial differences in their individual stories, the special few who prove themselves capable of achieving amazing comebacks are all doing the same thing, going through the same process to get up (to borrow Rodney's phrase) and get moving again, better than before. And although I made this discovery within the athletic realm, it applies elsewhere. Most of the remarkable men and women featured in these pages are athletes, but in many cases the defeats and challenges they came back from occurred outside the sporting context, and their comebacks themselves transcend sport.

My greatest hopes for this book are (1) that it is read by athletes and nonathletes alike and (2) that every reader is able to apply the inspiration and learning they glean from it to their own life, whether it be in a sport, a relationship, a job, a health crisis, or any other circumstance where a comeback is called for. If you happen to be an athlete, the stories I share here will have a special resonance. And if you aren't, then I encourage you to read *The Comeback Quotient* as one long metaphor (life as marathon, if you will), the same way businesspeople read Sun Tzu's *The Art of War* or Machiavelli's *The Prince*. Life really is a kind of marathon, and the secret to coming back from defeats and challenges is the same both on the racecourse and off—a secret you will soon know as fully as any champion.

1

THE ULTRAREALISTS

Reality is that which, when you stop believing in it, doesn't go away.

PHILIP K. DICK

I BECAME A FAN of Joan Benoit in a single instant—approximately 12:34 p.m. on April 18, 1983—when she strode past my roadside viewing position in Framingham, Massachusetts, on her way to winning the Boston Marathon in 2:22:43, a world-best time for women. Eleven years old at the time, I had come to Boston with my family to watch my father race, having never heard of Joan prior to that day. But when she flashed by me far ahead of all the other women in the race and behind only 120 of the nearly 6,000 men, I had a new hero. In movement, posture, and bearing, Joan radiated a fearless determination, her compact frame slanted forward at an aggressive angle, chin lifted in warriorlike confidence, eyes focused up the road predatorially, searching for runners to humble. I followed her exploits closely from that day forward.

Joan's next big race was the (first-ever) US Olympic Trials Women's Marathon, scheduled to take place on May 12, 1984, in Olympia, Washington. Having established herself as the greatest woman marathoner on the planet with her performance in Boston, she was favored to not only sail through the trials but to win gold in Los Angeles in August. But on March 16, Joan felt a sudden twinge in her right knee during a 20-mile training run near her home in Freeport, Maine. Within minutes, the pain had become so intense that her normally crisp stride degenerated into a ragged slog. Never before had she bailed out of a workout, so she wasn't sure whether or when to stop, but in the end the decision was made for her. At 17 miles, the leg stopped working altogether.

The timing of the injury couldn't have been worse. With the trials less than two months away, Joan could ill afford a major interruption to her preparations. Rest and cortisone injections brought only temporary relief, and on April 25, again unable to run, she flew to Portland, Oregon, to consult renowned orthopedic surgeon Stan James, who prescribed anti-inflammatory medication and more rest. Five days later, Joan started a test run with high hopes and finished it in tears, having survived just three miles. James then advised surgery, a last resort that Joan, who felt certain that *something* in her knee was restricting its natural movement, leapt at.

Seventeen days before the Olympic trials, James removed from Joan's knee a mass of fibrous material that, true to her intuition, was impeding the joint's normal operation. Putting prudence before fear of losing fitness, Joan dutifully waited 72 hours before testing the results of the procedure with a gentle pool run, which produced no pain. This was followed by a pain-free stationary bike ride the next day and a pain-free outdoor run the day after that. Not a moment too soon, Joan had renewed confidence and even a bit of momentum. But then, on the 3rd of May, just eight days before the trials, she got a little carried away on her final long run and strained her left hamstring, leaving her with no choice but to take yet another day off.

Joan arrived in Olympia having no clue what her body was capable of. Yet although Olympic qualification would require only a top-three finish, she still craved outright victory, in pursuit of which she seized the lead at 12 miles, hoping to demoralize her opponents and avoid a sprint finish, which had never been her specialty and was even less so now, given the touch-and-go state of her ailing hammy. In the middle third of the race, Joan stretched her lead out to 400 yards. Things were looking good, and when, at 17 miles, she spotted her anxious coach, Bob Sevene, on the curb, she assured him, "Sev, I'm all right."

Except she wasn't. At 20 miles, all those missed days of training came back to haunt her. Joan's legs turned to concrete, her pace slowing abruptly from 5:40 to 6:00 per mile. Then her hamstring, relatively quiet until that point, started screaming at her, and she slowed down even more. Smelling blood, Joan's closest chasers began to close the gap. Running on sheer will, Joan locked her mind on a single thought—*If they catch me, I'm dead*—and gutted out the final miles to win the trials by 37 seconds. Three months later, at the Los Angeles Olympics, a fully fit and healthy Joan Benoit became history's first female Olympic Marathon gold medalist.

Every sports fan loves a comeback. Muhammad Ali's breathtaking eighth-round knockout of a previously invincible George Foreman in 1974, restoring a heavyweight title stripped from him eight years earlier for Muhammad's defiance of a Vietnam War draft order. Monica Seles's gutsy victory at the 1996 Australian Open, three years after a horrific on-court knife attack that left her nursing psychic wounds far deeper than the gash in her right shoulder. Thirty-nine-year-old Tom Brady's surgical dismantling of the Atlanta Falcons' defense in the late stages of Super Bowl LI, delivering his New England Patriots almost single-handedly from a hopeless-seeming 28–3 deficit to overtime victory. Such feats appeal to a deeply human craving for proof that anything is possible—that it ain't over till it's over.

By the time Joan won gold, I was a runner myself, having become one exactly one day after I watched her streak past me in Framingham. A comeback means even more to a fellow athlete than it does to a mere fan. A fan looks at, say, Bethany Hamilton's improbable win at the 2016 NSSA National Championship two years after the young surfer's entire left arm was bitten off by a tiger shark and thinks, *Wow, that's amazing!* I looked at Joan Benoit's comeback from an 11th-hour breakdown to winning the 1984 US Olympic Trials Marathon and thought, *Wow, I want to be like that!*

While fans are content to be entertained and inspired by great comebacks, athletes want to emulate them, to borrow whatever special quality it is that enables a rare few to conquer when defeat seems certain. After all, a great comeback is nothing more than an extreme version of what we athletes try to do every day, which is to succeed where success doesn't come easily. That's the thing about sports: They're hard. The ancient Greek word for athletic competition is *agon*, which is the root of the English word *agony*. That's no accident. Training for and completing a marathon, for example, is agonizing, even if your goal isn't to win an Olympic gold medal and even if you don't injure your knee eight weeks before the big race.

Because sports are hard, it takes more than physical ability to succeed in them. Mental fitness is also required. While physical fitness enables an athlete to *do* hard things, mental fitness enables an athlete to *deal with* hard things, and no athlete realizes his or her full potential without both.

But what exactly is mental fitness? I define it as the ability to make the best of a bad situation—and in sports it's almost always a bad situation to some degree. The agony that athletes experience when training hard and competing is really a best-case scenario, or the worst that happens on a good day. And good days are somewhat rare. Most days, athletes are dealing with something beyond just garden-variety suffering, whether it's injury, illness, aging, overtraining, menstruation, the wrong diet, a bad workout, a bad performance, burnout, stagnating fitness, life stress, time pressure, weather, living in the wrong damn place for the lifestyle you've chosen—the list goes on.

Some athletes deal with this stuff better than others. Some time ago, I asked my Twitter followers—most of whom participate in endurance sports—to self-rate their mental fitness. Among the poll's 371 respondents, 13 percent confessed that their mind was "a major limiter," 28 percent rated their mental game as "average at best," 48 percent selected the "good, not great" option, and the remaining 11 percent claimed to have "Eliud Kipchoge level" mental fitness (a reference to Kenya's legendary marathon world-record smasher, renowned for his psychological fortitude). If my Twitter followers are representative of the broader athlete population, then nearly 90 percent of us are aware that the contents of our head are more of a liability than an asset, and given the well-known tendency of people to overestimate their aptitudes (83 percent of drivers rate themselves as more careful than average, for example), it's safe to say that just about every athlete other than Eliud Kipchoge himself could stand to improve in this area.

Most athletes have a pretty good idea how to improve their physical ability. It's a simple matter of following proven best practices in training. But very few have a clear understanding of how to improve their mental fitness. Some hire sports psychologists. Still others read books on the topic or practice visualization or journaling or use some other mental training tool suggested by a coach or peer or internet influencer. Still others just keep grinding along, hoping it happens on its own. Which way is best? And why does it matter?

Before we answer these questions, let's take a moment to consider why the path to *physical* improvement is so much better understood. Beginning in the early 2000s, exercise scientists began to rigorously study the training practices of elite athletes, particularly endurance athletes, eventually discovering striking consistencies across sport disciplines and geographical regions. Among these shared patterns is the 80/20 ratio of intensity distribution, where 80 percent of weekly training time is spent at low intensity and 20 percent at moderate to high intensity. Such consistencies are taken as evidence that, through generations of trial and error, elite endurance athletes have hit upon the training methods that are most effective in developing aerobic fitness in humans. Subsequent studies involving amateur athletes have determined that the same methods work equally well for mere mortals.

It stands to reason that what's true for physical ability is true for mental fitness, as well. If some ways of dealing with bad situations work better than others, and if one way works best, it seems likely that those athletes who deal with bad situations most successfully do so by means of the same, superior method—the psychological equivalent of the 80/20 rule, if you will.

Suppose it were your job to identify this method, if indeed it does exist. The obvious approach would be to replicate the process exercise scientists used to identify best practices on the physical side. Step one would be to collect a number of notable examples of athletes making the very best of the very worst situations. Step two would be to look for common themes among them. There's certainly no shortage of material to work with. Sports lore is rife with famous comebacks—stories of athletes overcoming tremendous challenges to achieve great things. Is there a thread that ties together all achievements of this sort? To find out, you must do more than just review the tape, so to speak. On their surface, these events reveal little about the underlying *how*. An athlete falls, gets back up, and wins. Resilience! Well, sure, I suppose. But to draw any kind of usable lesson from such examples, you need to dig beneath the surface and look at what was going on inside the athlete's head. Mental fitness is exercised within the mind, after all.

Sounds like a lot of work, doesn't it? Lucky for you, I've already done it. Ever since Joan Benoit achieved that gritty win in Olympia, I've been fascinated by comebacks. Later, when I became a professional endurance sports writer, I enjoyed numerous opportunities to talk to the athletes behind other great comebacks, get inside their heads, and learn more about how they had experienced them from the inside.

These interactions alone did not yield any great epiphanies, however. It's often difficult to perceive a feature that is ubiquitous in one group unless you've got another group to compare it against. For me, that group has been the recreational endurance athletes I've coached since 2001. Two decades of working with everyday athletes in the morning and writing about exceptional athletes in the afternoon, as it were, has taught me that, in most respects, the two groups are similar. Both are passionate, tough, and intelligent. But there is a key difference between them.

Simply put, athletes who fail to make the best of a bad situation *turn away from reality*, whereas athletes capable of achieving great comebacks face reality squarely. I know what you might be thinking: *Huh?* And believe me, I get it. Of all the possible psychological discrepancies between everyday and exceptional athletes I might have noticed, this isn't the one I expected, either. But, having noticed it, I can't unnotice it.

When athletes with less than Kipchoge-level mental fitness find themselves in a bad situation, all too often they fail to accept it as real; or, having accepted it, they fail to embrace that new reality; or, having embraced it, they fail to do what's necessary to address it. In fact, failure to make the best of a bad situation *never happens for any other reason*. Every time an athlete I work with fails to make the best of a bad situation, I can trace the cause back to one of these three steps not taken.

Athletes capable of achieving great comebacks are different. Some of them work with sports psychologists, and some don't. Some read books on mental fitness, and some don't. Some practice techniques like visualization and journaling, and some don't. But every one of them faces reality in bad situations. This three-step process of accepting, embracing, and addressing reality is the sine qua non of great athletic comebacks—the one thing that athletes with the highest level of mental fitness do to overcome major challenges. For the rest of us, gaining mental fitness entails nothing more and nothing less than getting better at this process by following the example set by these "ultrarealists."

ULTRAREALISTS IN ACTION

The idea that the essence of mental fitness is a certain orientation toward reality may be new, but there is plenty to back it up. A brief look at three notable athletic comebacks offers a clearer picture of what it means to be an ultrarealist, which we'll build on later.

Comeback #1: Geoffrey Kamworor

The 2016 World Half Marathon Championships in Cardiff, Wales, were hotly anticipated by running fans as a grudge match between British legend Mo Farah and Kenyan upstart Geoffrey Kamworor. It wasn't just the credentials of the two men that generated so much excitement for the showdown (though they certainly were a major factor, Mo having amassed five world championship titles and two Olympic gold medals at 5000 and 10,000 meters, while Geoffrey came into the race as its defending champion and a two-time world champion in cross country). It was also the public smack talk Geoffrey had engaged in before the race, the 23-year-old Kenyan going so far as to guarantee Sir Mo's defeat in one interview. Such bravado was especially brazen given the fact that Geoffrey had never beaten Mo in head-to-head competition, not to mention the fact that the World Half Marathon Championships were taking place on Mo's home turf.

The weather on race morning was of the sort that Brits like Mo are accustomed to and most African runners are not: chilly, wet, and blustery. This may explain why, when the starting pistol sounded, Geoffrey's left foot slipped out from under him and he sprawled face-first onto the slick tarmac, where he lay for seven long and terrifying seconds as the 16,000 amateur runners behind him began to trample him underfoot and Mo sped away with the other contenders.

As chance would have it, one of the runners in Geoffrey's immediate vicinity at the moment of this absurdly awful start was Oliver Williams, a 30-year-old Welshman who was attempting to set a new Guinness World Record for the fastest half-marathon ever run in a Superman costume. To aid the ratifying process, Oliver wore (in addition to a red cape and an "S" on his chest) a head-mounted GoPro that captured the newly risen Geoffrey as he elbowed his way past the ersatz Man of Steel and slalomed between slower runners in reckless pursuit of the race leaders.

Within three minutes he caught them, having blitzed the first kilometer at 4:00-mile pace. The effort took its toll, however. Normally an aggressive frontrunner, the oxygen-starved challenger to Mo Farah's supremacy tucked in behind him for the next several miles, gathering his strength instead of setting the pace. A slow attrition ensued, struggling runners falling off one by one. Mo lost contact just shy of the halfway mark, and by 11 miles the race was down to two men: Geoffrey's countryman Bedan Karoki and, incredibly, Geoffrey himself, who surged away to a 26-second victory.

Comeback #2: Mirinda Carfrae

In October 2014, Mirinda Carfrae arrived on the Big Island of Hawaii as the odds-on favorite to win the pro women's division of the Ironman® World Championship, and for good reason. The 33-year-old Australian had smashed the event record in claiming the previous year's title and had shown no sign of regressing since then, winning the ultracompetitive Challenge Roth triathlon in July with one of the fastest women's iron-distance times in history. In a prerace interview with espnW.com, Mirinda conceded that anything less than victory would be a disappointment.

Imagine how she must have felt, then, to find herself in eighth place at the bike-run transition, more than 14 minutes behind race leader Daniela Ryf of Switzerland. No athlete had ever overcome such a large deficit to win in Kona, a fact that the reigning champion was well aware of, saying afterward, "I didn't believe I was going to win. I had to let go of that hope. So I figured I'd try to put together the very best race that I could and change my goal from winning to getting in the top five."

In pursuit of this more modest ambition, Mirinda blasted out of the bike-run transition at 6:30 per mile, exceeding her own course-record pace. Despite the aggressive tempo, she managed to pass only two other women in the first half of the marathon. But then, at 14 miles, Mirinda scored a three-for-one, overtaking a trio of competitors in the span of seconds and sliding into third place. Just like that, plan A was back on the table.

Conscious of the need to tamp down her rising excitement, the pint-size Aussie concentrated on making smart decisions, such as slowing down just enough to get the fluid and calories she required at aid stations instead of barreling through to save seconds. Her reward was another victim, Britain's Rachel Joyce, who ceded second place to Mirinda at 20 miles. By now Daniela Ryf was visible ahead, and the final outcome a fait accompli. Mirinda grabbed the lead at 23 miles and went on to consummate the greatest come-from-behind victory in the 36-year history of the Ironman World Championship.

Comeback #3: Joan Benoit

As you know already, Joan Benoit suffered a significant knee injury during a training run in March 1984, yet went on to win the US Olympic Trials Women's Marathon just eight weeks later. Subsequent events would demonstrate that Joan's miracle in Olympia was no fluke. In 1991, she returned from two pregnancies and a three-year hiatus from elite competition to complete the Boston Marathon in 2:26:42, the fastest marathon run by an American woman that year. Seventeen years later, at age 50, Joan qualified for and competed in the US Olympic Trials Marathon, setting an age-group world record with her finish time of 2:49:09. Joan Benoit Samuelson (as she is now known) is living proof that great athletic comebacks aren't so much a matter of stars aligning as they are something that certain people are able to do, regardless of how the heavens behave.

ANATOMY OF A COMEBACK

The comebacks I've just described were enthusiastically celebrated by sports fans and journalists. Oliver Williams's video of Geoffrey Kamworor's mad dash through the masses in Wales elicited gushing expressions of awe ("Wow!" "Impressive!") from many viewers. *New York Times* reporter Peter Alfano described Joan Benoit as "better on one leg than the other 237 qualifiers were on two" in his write-up of the '84 trials marathon. And Ironman World Championship announcer Mike Reilly pronounced Mirinda Carfrae's performance "simply unbelievable!" as she crossed the finish line in 2014.

What's missing from these reactions is any substantive discussion about or understanding of *why* these comebacks are so remarkable. In Alfanso's praise there is a hint that he regarded Joan's comeback as a display of astonishing physical ability. She was so good at running, he suggests, that she was able to win the trials marathon despite her disastrous lead-up to it. Similarly, we may infer, Geoffrey's comeback was seen as proof that he was so good at running that he was able to win despite falling down and Mirinda so good at running that she was able to win despite getting off her bike more than 14 minutes behind Daniela Ryf.

Unquestionably, these athletes could not have pulled off their respective comebacks without supreme physical ability. But remember, physical ability merely allows an athlete to do hard things, whereas mental fitness is required to deal with hard things, and Geoffrey, Joan, and Mirinda all had to deal with some very hard things to win their races. Each did so by facing reality in circumstances where most of us would turn away from it.

When a situation turns bad, the first opportunity an athlete is presented with is the opportunity to accept or not accept the reality of it, and it's an opportunity you don't want to miss. Acceptance is absolutely essential to making the best of the situation. Why? Because to accept a bad situation is to perceive it in a way that preserves your ability to make choices. But acceptance isn't always easy. Failure to accept reality, on the other hand, is quite a bit easier. It happens in two ways. The first is panic, where a bad turn of events is perceived as so unacceptable that instinct takes over and the athlete acts reflexively, allowing the situation to control them instead of making free choices on how to deal with it. A somewhat milder version of panic is catastrophizing, where an athlete perceives a bad situation as worse than it actually is or decides it's all over before it really is. The second way of failing to accept reality is the exact opposite of panic/catastrophizing: denial, where an athlete minimizes a bad situation or pretends it doesn't even exist.

We've all heard the expression, "When life gives you lemons, make lemonade." This homespun wisdom is really just another way of saying, "When you find yourself in a bad situation, acknowledge it and make the best of it." Accepting reality means recognizing that life has given you lemons—nothing more, nothing less—and not wasting time and energy on wishing it hadn't.

Many athletes in Geoffrey Kamworor's place would have panicked, either curling into a ball with their arms covering their head or scrambling to safety at the side of the road. Others would have catastrophized the situation by continuing the race but without hope, viewing it as lost before it really was. Geoffrey did neither of these things. Almost as if he'd had advance warning about what was going to happen and had steeled himself for it, he accepted the reality exactly as it was: a seven-second delay compounded by a few bumps and bruises and a couple of hundred human obstacles he needed to get around to erase the deficit.

An injury such as the one Joan Benoit suffered eight weeks before the Olympic trials is no easier to accept. A lot of athletes slip into a fear-driven denial state in these situations. Terrified of throwing away their hard-earned fitness, they pretend the injury doesn't exist and try to train through it, with predictable consequences. Joan, too, was terrified of losing fitness, but she did not allow her fear to cloud her judgment or make the decisions for her. Acknowledging the severity of her injury, she bailed out of runs when necessary, took more than 15 days off from running in the final two months before the trials, and came up with a plan B of trying to qualify for the Olympics on the track if she couldn't run the marathon, which helped reduce the temptation to take foolish risks.

Mirinda Carfrae did something analogous when she got off the bike at the Ironman World Championship and learned that she was nearly a quarter of an hour behind Daniela Ryf. Calculating that she would have to complete the marathon in an unheard-of 2:47 to overtake Ryf before the finish line, she acknowledged to herself that she had virtually no chance of winning. But instead of giving up (the panic/catastrophizing response) or lying to herself and attempting to run a 2:47 marathon (the denial response), she accepted the math and immediately moved on to step two in the process of making the best of a bad situation, which entails embracing reality by committing to making the lemons you've been given into lemonade, so to speak.

Not every athlete who accepts the reality of a bad situation takes this next step. Acceptance of an unwanted reality often leads to demoralization or apathy—a "What's the point?" attitude. When a situation turns bad, it is natural to wish that what is happening were not happening. Too often, though, we get stuck in this state of mind, thereby sealing off any possibility of making the best of the situation, whereas ultrarealists quickly pivot from wishing things were different to resolving to *make* them different, even if their original goal is out of reach.

It so happens that I experienced something akin to Geoffrey Kamworor's Cardiff mishap at the start of the 1987 New England High School Cross Country Championships, hitting the deck mere steps into my race. I wasn't on the ground long, losing maybe three or four seconds to the rest of the field, but I never recovered mentally from the incident. Running rattled the rest of the way, I finished 66th in a race where I should have cracked the top 25. In short, I failed to embrace the situation—unlike Geoffrey, who, in a much bigger race with a lot more at stake, was able to quickly pivot from wishing he hadn't fallen to forgetting that he'd fallen.

The mindset that enables ultrarealists to embrace bad situations was well described by Joan Benoit in her 1987 autobiography *Running Tide*. "My philosophy of running is, I don't dwell on it, I do it," she wrote. Sounds easy enough, but this mindset was severely tested by her knee injury, with Joan coming close to packing her bags and flying home to Maine not once but twice during her period of limbo in Oregon. I think it's safe to say that many athletes in her shoes would have gone ahead and packed, but Joan's ability to treat her hard luck as a challenge rather than as a disappointment was just enough to stop her each time.

Mirinda Carfrae showed the same ability in Kona when she adjusted her goal from winning to cracking the top five. The fact that she did end up winning is beside the point. What matters is that she ran the best race she was capable of on a tough day by embracing her situation and spontaneously coming up with as much midrace enthusiasm for a top-five finish as she'd previously had to win—a salvaging of morale that, again safe to say, few athletes in comparable positions could pull off.

Returning to our lemons-to-lemonade metaphor, the third step in the process of making the best of a bad situation entails actually making lemonade from the lemons you've been given. Getting through the prior steps does not, after all, guarantee that something drinkable will be produced. Athletes who get this far are frequently derailed by failures of effort and failures of judgment—two more ways of turning away from reality.

At a press conference held after the 2016 World Half Marathon Championship, Geoffrey Kamworor told reporters, "It was really tough after that fall to catch up, but I fought hard." I smile every time I read this banal description of what must have been an absolute sufferfest for the young Kenyan. Physical ability was only one reason it was possible for him to win despite his fall, even after he'd committed to the effort. The other was Geoffrey's willingness to endure exquisite misery in the process. Other athletes for whom a similar comeback was also just barely possible and who both accepted and embraced this reality might very well have given up during the process only because the suffering required was too great—or, put another way, because what was actually possible *felt* impossible.

Science has demonstrated that some athletes have a higher tolerance for pain and suffering than others do, and that those who have a higher tolerance are more accepting of these sensations. It's not that they feel them less; rather, they avoid compounding their pain and suffering by wishing they weren't happening, a rejection of reality that adds a layer of emotional unpleasantness to the raw physical sensations. The same willingness to face reality that allows certain athletes to accept a negative turn of events also helps them bear what must be borne to address the bad situation.

FLOWCHART OF FACING REALITY

This flowchart summarizes the three steps involved in making the best of a bad situation and the specific ways in which choosing to either face or turn away from your present reality affects the outcome.

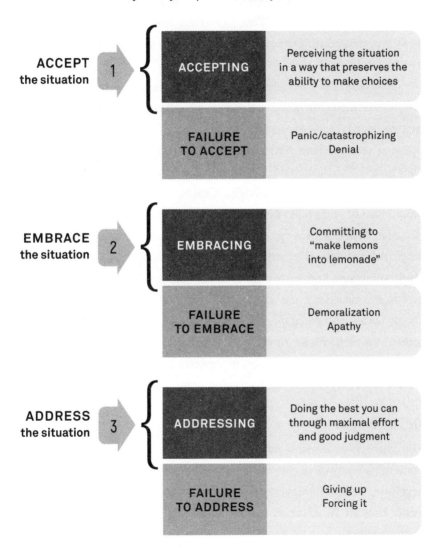

Joan Benoit described this feature of ultrarealism perfectly in her memoir, writing, "People ask how I can run with pain or keep working toward a goal that seems hopelessly distant. If I want to run a marathon faster than I've run in the past, I have to cope with the discomfort that sometimes accompanies long-distance running. I know the end result will be worth the effort." Her matter-of-fact willingness to face reality, as much as her talent, is what permitted Joan to run better on one leg than her competition did on two legs in Olympia.

Addressing a bad situation is not all about tolerance for pain and suffering, however. Judgment plays a role as well. Bad situations are problems, and not every problem can be solved by brute force. Identifying the right solution to a problem often requires an athlete to let the bad situation they're in talk to them, to be receptive to their present reality's textures and contours and willing to improvise in response to what they receive. This is what Mirinda Carfrae did during the run leg of that Ironman World Championship. Where another athlete who accepted and embraced her situation might have addressed it by sheer effort, Mirinda addressed it through smart decisions on pacing, nutrition, and emotional self-regulation. In other words, she picked the real solution rather than the simple one.

By now, it should be clear that the process of making the best of a bad situation is all about facing reality, and that every possible way of failing to make the best of a bad situation is a matter of turning away from reality. So, are you ready to get real?

GETTING REAL

Ultrarealists like Geoffrey Kamworor, Joan Benoit, and Mirinda Carfrae have something many of us don't—an extraordinary readiness to face reality—and if you want to fulfill your own potential, you want that too. But can you really have it? What if this special "comeback quotient" is innate rather than acquired?

I'll level with you: I think it is innate—to a degree. Certain genes are known, for example, to predispose a person toward anxiety, and if you're unfortunate enough to have inherited these genes, you may never be as cool under fire as the ultrarealists. This is no cause for despair, however. After all, we know that physical ability is also partly innate, and that no amount of training can make an athlete with average talent as fit as an athlete with elite talent who trains equally. Yet we also know that any one of us can get a hell of a lot fitter by following proven best practices in training over an extended period of time. The same is true of mental fitness.

I've seen it happen over and over again in my work with athletes. The coaching process is all about helping athletes deal with the various bad situations that are the very fabric of sport—everything from fitness plateaus to pre-competition anxiety. Some of these situations, such as loss of motivation, are entirely psychological in nature, while others, such as injury, have both physical and psychological components. Ever since I hit upon the idea that facing reality is how mental fitness operates, I have been highly intentional about coaxing athletes toward accepting, embracing, and addressing reality in the bad situations they encounter. And what I've found is that not only does this approach solve immediate problems, but over time it also leads to general gains in mental fitness.

A good example is Evan, a runner I coached a few years ago when he was in the midst of a middle-age comeback that followed a 20-year hiatus from competitive running. Like most of the athletes I work with, Evan came to me with a problem, which in his case was a tendency to push too hard in workouts and races that had left him literally unable to walk for an entire week after his most recent race.

Despite his awareness that he needed to stop forcing things, Evan didn't think he could learn to back off on his own, and I soon saw why. Time after time, he started the runs I planned for him with every intention of not pushing too hard and ended up doing so anyway, by—to be frank—bullshitting himself. On one occasion, I pointed out to Evan that he had once again drifted into zone 3 (moderate intensity) during a long run that was supposed to have been done entirely in zone 2 (low intensity). His defense was that the lapse had occurred on a downhill section of the route he'd chosen, and he figured that running downhill in zone 3 was less stressful than running either uphill or on flat ground in zone 3, and thus, he contended, he hadn't really defied the spirit of the workout.

"Zone 3 is zone 3, Evan," I said. "And you know it."

This is just one example of the many small ways in which I wouldn't let Evan get away with not facing reality. And although each instance alone didn't accomplish much, their cumulative effect was significant. After several weeks of working together, Evan began to hear my voice in his head during runs, calling bullshit on him right when he was about to commit another lapse, and as a result he became more compliant in respecting his zones. Within a few more weeks, he no longer needed this crutch—it was his own voice he heard steering his self-deceptive instincts back to reality.

The process didn't stop there. Facing reality is more than just something you do or fail to do in a given moment; it's also a mindset. You might start off practicing it only for the sake of solving one specific problem, but through this practice you gradually shift your entire orientation toward reality, becoming readier to accept, embrace, and address reality when facing other problems. This is what happened with Evan.

By training himself to quickly catch these moments of self-deception, Evan became more honest with himself generally. This evolution, in turn, led him to discover a deep well of anger and self-loathing that he had carried inside since a difficult childhood and was the cause of his tendency to use running as a form of self-punishment. It didn't happen overnight, but over time Evan got to the point where he could accept this part of himself without letting it run the show—or sabotage his running.

About a year after I stopped working with Evan, he emailed me to share the news that he had just run the best race of his life and to thank me for the role he felt I'd played in making it possible. "During the race," he wrote, "the standard self-doubt stuff came up, and my normal response, in a race of this length, is to push harder and start putting my pacing as the number-one priority for my conscious brain. This time, instead of doing that, I felt a connection to a different part of myself. The only way I can really describe it is confidence, but not arrogant confidence. It felt more like a confident me holding space for all my insecurities to come and be heard but also reassured that everything is under control."

This sense of control is the essence of what it feels like to be an ultrarealist. When you've cultivated the ability to fully accept, embrace, and address any situation, you are no longer dependent on external circumstances. While you still want things to go your way, it no longer really matters if they do or don't. In either case, you know you'll be able to make the best of the situation. You're in control of the only thing you truly can control, which is your mind, and it feels like freedom.

THE ROAD AHEAD

The approach I use to help athletes like Evan make the best of bad situations is based on reality therapy, which you will learn more about in the next chapter. One of the things I like about this approach is its rootedness in the normal problem-solving experience that athletes are already constantly engaged in. It eschews diagnosis of conditions or hang-ups. There are no particular mental exercises prescribed. You don't even need to think of it as a way to build mental fitness. Instead, you can just think of it as a way to make the best of the next bad situation you find yourself in, and the next, and the next. And you don't need a coach to practice it. All that's required is that you enter into each new challenge with the conscious intention of accepting, embracing, and addressing reality and with an understanding of precisely what it means to do these things. It couldn't be simpler.

As Thelonious Monk said, though, "Simple ain't easy." The instincts that cause us to turn away from reality in bad situations are powerful and not easily tamed. I will do my best in the pages ahead to equip you with tools that will help you handle each new challenge a little better than the last one. In the next chapter, I'll make the case that ultrarealism is the true essence of mental fitness, with support from ancient philosophy, cutting-edge science, and much in between. I'll then guide you through the three steps involved in making the best of a bad situation—accepting reality, embracing reality, and addressing reality—with further examples of how ultrarealists do each of these things. In Chapters 6 through 8, we'll explore the most common types of bad situation that athletes experience—the bad break, the rude awakening, and self-sabotage—and identify the strategies and methods that ultrarealists use to come back from each. The concluding chapter looks at what happens when comebacks fail, and in so doing reveals what ultrarealism is really for, which is not guaranteeing success but making your athletic and life journeys richer and more meaningful than they would otherwise be, win or lose.

Be prepared. Even with the tools and inspiration of the ultrarealists at your disposal, the road ahead will include many missteps. Time and again you will fail to make the best of a bad situation, either by not accepting an unwanted reality, or by not embracing a reality you've accepted, or by not addressing a reality you've accepted and embraced. Your next opportunity to do better will come soon, though, and if you "keep showing up" (to borrow a phrase made popular by American runner and ultrarealist Desiree Linden after she won the Boston Marathon in her seventh attempt), your hard work will be richly rewarded. Whether or not you ever become a full-fledged ultrarealist capable of pulling off legendary comebacks, each step forward in this journey will make you a calmer, stronger, and more self-trusting individual who makes better choices and achieves more satisfying outcomes in sport and in life. How do I know this? Because I'm on the same road myself.

11 MONTHS TO SANTA ROSA

I swam today—my first lap swim in almost nine years. It wasn't much of a workout—just a slow, steady half-mile at a local health club I joined exclusively for its 25-yard indoor pool—but it's a start.

The reason I haven't swum in nine years is that I don't particularly enjoy swimming, and I don't enjoy it because I'm not very good at it. So I avoid the pool except when I'm training for triathlons, and I haven't done a triathlon since September 2009. But I've decided to make a comeback as a triathlete, and have signed up for a race. Hence today's swim.

The race I've chosen is Ironman Santa Rosa, which will take place next May, almost 11 months from now. That's a long time to train for a triathlon, even an Ironman, but I'm going to need every single day I've got to get ready. My rust in the pool is the least of the obstacles I'll have to overcome just to make it to the start line, let alone achieve my goals. My last attempt at a triathlon comeback nine years ago fizzled when I developed chronic knee pain while training for Ironman Arizona. Ever since then, the pain has returned any time I've attempted to ride more than three or four hours a week, and I'm all but certain it will do so again in the weeks ahead unless I'm able to find a fix. Past efforts to solve the issue, which have included switching pedals and fiddling with seat height, have failed entirely.

A separate injury is affecting my running. Ten months ago I suffered a severe hip abductor tendon strain while training for the Chicago Marathon. I recovered quickly and even managed to set a new personal best, but I reinjured the tendon 12 weeks later and have been going in circles with it for the past six months, taking time off, easing back into running, experiencing a setback, taking time off, and so on. Last week I bailed out of an easy eight-miler when the pain in my groin reached red-flag level, and I am currently doing all of my run training on a treadmill, at a steep incline, and it's actually not running at all but brisk walking.

Heck of a time to stage a comeback, right? But I have my reasons. My one prior Ironman was in Wisconsin in 2002. I completed it in 10:13:15, missing out on qualifying for the world championship in Kona by 23 seconds. My "A" goal for my comeback race in Santa Rosa is to qualify for Kona in my age group (I'll turn

48 a week before the event), which will probably require a finish time under 9:50 given how competitive the sport has become since I last competed in it. My "B" goal is to break 10 hours, and my "C" goal is to improve upon my previous Ironman time. In short, I am setting a high bar for myself, an absurdly high bar, you might say, in light of my situation, and yet I wouldn't have it any other way.

You see, my true ambition has less to do with achieving these goals and more to do with how I pursue them. I certainly do want to qualify for Kona and to break 10 hours, but what I want even more is to chase these goals as an ultrarealist would. The purpose of this book is to help endurance athletes become more mentally fit by getting better at facing reality in difficult situations. As a competitive endurance athlete myself, and as one who truly believes that accepting, embracing, and addressing reality is what it takes to succeed in the face of major challenges, I'd be a fool not to aim for the ultrarealist standard in my own training and racing. In attempting to do so throughout this triathlon comeback, I hope not only to experience a more rewarding journey but also to offer proof that you need not be a world-class talent to be an ultrarealist.

In one sense, I've been on this journey for a while already, exploring the psychology of endurance sports and working to strengthen my mental game since my twenties. But ultrarealism as a distinct and cohesive concept took shape in my mind only recently, and my embryonic triathlon comeback is my first chance to test it. Concepts matter. There's a huge difference, for example, between having a general intention of being a good Boy Scout and consciously adhering to the Scout's Oath in one's daily conduct. Up to this point in my athletic life, I've had a general intention to practice the various mental performance skills I've picked up over the years. But in my current quest, I will consciously adhere to what I think of as the Ultrarealist's Creed: "Accept, embrace, and address reality in every situation, no matter how bad it is."

Already this shift in mindset is making a difference. Were I not living by the Ultrarealist's Creed, I'd be wasting a lot more energy right now worrying about my present physical limitations. Instead I have kept my focus on the following realities: (1) I have plenty of time to improve my swimming. (2) It is unlikely that the problem with my right knee represents a permanent barrier to doing the amount of quality bike riding I'll need to do to achieve my goals. And (3) my running is sure to come around if I show a little patience and resist making an abrupt leap into 100 percent training when I'm only 90 percent ready.

In clearly distinguishing in my mind what I can control from what I can't, and by casting out of mind what I can't control, I can say for sure that I am, at the very least, enjoying my triathlon comeback more than I might otherwise be at this early stage. Whether modeling my thinking and behavior after the ultrarealists in this way and others yields better results, only time will tell.

2

DISCOVERING WHAT
WE'VE ALWAYS KNOWN

The human capacity for self-deception knows no bounds.

ROBERT TRIVERS

KATE COURTNEY'S NEW YEAR'S RESOLUTION for 2018 was to meditate every morning. The meditation part of this pledge was nothing new; Kate had meditated on and off since college. It was the every-morning part that demanded a special commitment from the 22-year-old professional mountain biker. Determined to keep the practice going this time, yet also wise enough to know that sheer willpower wouldn't get the job done, she put in place a few key measures (such as banishing her cell phone from her bedroom at night) that made the ritual just that—a ritual rather than the chore it had sometimes become in the past. It worked.

There's more than one way to meditate. Kate chose mindfulness meditation, which entails emptying the mind of the chatter that normally occupies it and focusing on the raw perceptions that constitute the foundation of our experience of the present moment. In other words, mindfulness meditation is all about receiving reality openly, just as it is, without filters. Sometimes, for a little variety, Kate sat while listening to guided meditations by Jon Kabat-Zinn, author of *Full Catastrophe Living* and creator of the

Stress Reduction Clinic at the University of Massachusetts Medical School. Kabat-Zinn's research has shown that mindfulness training can reduce stress and improve overall mental well-being by cultivating the ability to accept and embrace the "full catastrophe" of life and to waste less time and energy wishing things were different.

Right away, Kate noticed a dramatic improvement in the quality of her sleep. As time passed, she began to experience additional benefits, including heightened self-awareness—an ability to take a mental step back from her own consciousness in certain situations and choose more helpful thoughts, emotions, and actions instead of simply reacting to things.

What remained to be seen was how this newfound independence from external circumstances would affect Kate on the racecourse. Unfortunately, the 2018 season had scarcely begun when she suffered a knee injury during an altitude camp in Lake Tahoe that brought her training to an abrupt halt, forcing her to skip an event in Southern California and throwing her European World Cup racing plans into jeopardy. With the help of her support team, Kate was able to bounce back fairly quickly, but despite cramming two weeks' worth of training into the final week of her camp, she boarded a flight to Trentino, Italy, for the Val di Sole World Cup in early July feeling underprepared and uncertain of her fitness.

Most athletes in Kate's position would have been pretty worried. Kate herself would have been worried if she'd been in the same situation a year earlier. But meditation had taught her to adopt an attitude of gratitude in testing moments, and she did so during the long flight east, reminding herself that, as she later put it in a blog post, "Just a few weeks ago, I was sitting on the couch with ice on my knee with no idea when I'd be able to ride again," whereas now, "I was on my way to one of the most beautiful places in the world with an opportunity to do what I do best."

The same attitude carried over to the race itself. Where the "old" Kate might have brooded on the fact that she had no chance whatsoever of vying for a podium finish, as she was accustomed to doing, the "new" Kate chose to see herself as *fresher* than her opponents rather than less fit, and to embrace the day as a chance to practice racing intelligently. Straddling her bike on the start line, she felt calm and free of pressure. When the horn sounded, she set out cautiously, taking satisfaction in making up for her lack of preparation by paying extra attention to hydration and fueling, recovering on descents, and saving something for the last lap. As it turned out, that something she saved vaulted her past Elisabeth Brandau of Germany in the final stretch to capture seventh place, a result she would have considered a disappointment in other circumstances but now savored as a major mental victory.

As Kate continued with her meditation practice, her capacity to use her mind to her own competitive advantage increased further. In another blog post she wrote, "If I'm having a tough race and lose a few positions . . . I might shift my focus to something I can control—committing myself to doing all the technical features really well on this lap, or focusing on hitting my lines really smoothly, or even passing just one person. It's these small things that help me regain my rhythm, which can often make a big difference in a long race."

At the 2018 UCI Mountain Biking World Championship, held on September 8 in Lenzerheide, Switzerland, Kate found herself in second place after six of seven laps, trailing Annika Langvad of Denmark by 20 seconds. The natural temptation of any competitor in such a situation is to focus on the athlete ahead, but Kate stuck to her plan of executing a gold medal ride, not riding for a gold medal, and it paid off. Having once again saved something for the last lap, she caught Annika with fewer than eight minutes of riding left in the 95-minute race. Flustered, the Danish rider got careless, catching her front tire on an exposed tree root, and was forced to unclip a shoe and touch down briefly. Kate, meanwhile, continued to ride as if she were all by herself in search of her own best performance, powering past her opponent without a glance to become the first American cross-country mountain biking world champion in 17 years.

THE FIRST ULTRAREALISTS

Don't worry. I'm not trying to sell you on meditation. It's just one tool among many that Kate Courtney might have used to increase her mental fitness, or her ability to make the best of bad situations by facing reality.

To my knowledge, I am the first and only student of sport to define mental fitness in this way. If I were you, I would be very reluctant to pursue an approach to building mental fitness that only one person on earth believed in, no matter who he was. But I'm not asking you to do this either. The core wisdom upon which my definition of mental fitness is based has actually been around for millennia and has been articulated in various ways by spiritual leaders, philosophers, psychologists—and, yes, coaches and athletes. What's more, in recent years the conceptual foundation of what I call ultrarealism has been validated in unexpected ways through cutting-edge research in neuroscience and even physics. My goal in this chapter is to demonstrate to you that, specific terminology notwithstanding, I am in fact far from alone in believing that mental fitness consists in the ability to make the best of bad situations by accepting, embracing, and addressing reality, and to thereby persuade you that becoming an ultrarealist is a worthwhile undertaking for you.

There's a reason I started off with Kate Courtney's story about using meditation to get better at facing reality. The first known proponent of ultrarealism (to use my term) just so happens to be the same person who popularized mindfulness meditation. According to legend, the man we call the Buddha was born Siddhartha Gautama in the sixth century B.C.E. in the Himalayan foothills. Of royal blood, Siddhartha was raised by an overprotective father (we know nothing about his mother) who tried to shield him from suffering of all forms. It worked okay for a while, but when Siddhartha came of age, he began to range beyond the coddling confines of his home, and in a short span he witnessed three things that shook him deeply: a sick man, an old man, and a corpse. Ironically, it was precisely because Siddhartha had been sheltered from life's unpleasant parts that he was unprepared to handle these unpleasant images. As a result, he flipped out, fleeing his native village in search of a solution to the problem of human suffering.

It took some time, and there were a few missteps along the way, but in the end, through meditation, Siddhartha achieved an epiphany, and with it, inner peace. His key insight was that yearning, or wishing things were different than they are, is the root of all suffering, and that letting go of this desire is the secret to happiness. A famous line from the Buddhist scriptures, known as sutras, is the Sanskrit phrase "drishta dharma sukha viharin," which translates as "dwelling happily in things as they are." Mindfulness meditation became the main instrument in the Buddha's program for letting go of earthly attachments because he'd found that it trained the mind to be purely, passively receptive to whatever might be happening at a given moment.

Let's be clear: In postulating that wishing things were different is the root of all suffering, and that learning to accept reality is the secret to happiness, the Buddha was either right or wrong. If he was right, then surely other wise individuals would arrive at the same conclusion. And that's precisely what happened. The Stoic philosophers of the third century B.C.E., for example, although they used different language and concepts, articulated the same key insight the Buddha had taught some 300 years earlier.

The father of Stoicism was Zeno of Citium. According to his posthumous biographer, Diogenes Laërtius, Zeno grew up on Cyprus but arrived at Athens as a young man via shipwreck, a misfortune that he bore, well, stoically, reportedly saying afterward, "Now that I've been shipwrecked, I'm on a good journey." The same mindset would come to characterize the philosophy he developed in Athens and promulgated through daily open-air lectures. Although none of his own writings survive, through Diogenes we know that Zeno defined happiness as "a good flow of life," by which he meant a life that aligned with nature. Our modern definition of the word "stoicism" as indifference to pain and misfortune derives from this concept of going with nature's flow, or *kathekon*, as Zeno called it. In his view, nature was perfect, and therefore everything that happened was right and proper. Better, then, to change our minds to fit reality than to try to change reality to fit our minds. "Man conquers the world by conquering himself," Zeno preached.

Stoicism lasted well into the second century c.e., its tenets evolving as they passed from one major thinker to the next. Among the last great Stoics was Epictetus, whose particular take on the tradition was influenced by his life experience. Born into slavery, Epictetus suffered a crippling leg injury as a youth in Rome yet nevertheless managed to bootstrap his way to emancipation as an adult by dint of his prodigious intellectual gifts. Going a step further than Zeno, he taught that no person has any real control over external events and that those who desire to live a good life should focus entirely on controlling their mind. Like Zeno, Epictetus left behind no writings that survived, but a dedicated pupil recorded many of his sayings, which have been compiled in a classic book titled *The Art of Living*. My personal favorite is this nugget: "Man is not worried by real problems so much as by his imagined anxieties about real problems."

The idea that solving real problems requires first accepting and embracing them pops up again and again in subsequent philosophies. One example is transcendentalism, which flourished in the United States in the middle of the 19th century. "Self-Reliance," an essay penned in 1841 by Ralph Waldo Emerson, the man most closely associated with this tradition, ought perhaps to be required reading for any aspiring ultrarealist. In it, Emerson cautions us against allowing ourselves to be dependent on things going our way in the world. "A political victory, a rise in rents, the recovery of your sick, or the return of your absent friend, or some other favorable event, raises your spirits," he wrote, "and you think good days are preparing for you. Do not believe it. Nothing can bring you peace but yourself."

ULTRAREALISM IN SPORT

Sports are a microcosm of life. As such, they test people in similar ways, and the same qualities that enable people to master life's vicissitudes enable them to also master athletic challenges. It was inevitable, therefore, that the athletic world would produce its own ultrarealist philosophers. Among the earliest and most compelling of these is Percy Cerutty, an Australian running coach who took an unusual path toward becoming one of the sport's most iconic figures.

Born in 1895, Cerutty endured an abysmal childhood. Before he'd even seen his first birthday, he nearly died of food poisoning. Soon thereafter, his mother left his alcoholic father, taking their six children with her, and the rest of his childhood was spent in severe poverty. Chronically malnourished, Cerutty did not eat fruit of any kind until his teens, suffering double pneumonia (which left him with permanent lung damage) and other ailments as a consequence. At the outbreak of World War I, he was, to the surprise of no one, declared medically unfit to serve, and his health only got worse from there, digestive issues and migraine headaches adding themselves to his list of maladies.

At age 43, mired in a humdrum career as a postal worker, Cerutty suffered a complete physical and mental breakdown and was forced to take a six-month leave of absence from work, during which his weight dropped to 99 pounds. One of his doctors told Cerutty he'd be dead within two years. But another doctor had a different take, challenging the patient to choose his own destiny. "You have to save yourself," he admonished. "If you want to do anything about yourself, you'll get out of that bed under your own will and spirit."

For whatever reason, these words touched a match to a hidden cache of strength in Cerutty's soul, igniting an astonishing personal comeback. Getting out of bed was only the beginning. In the weeks and months that followed, Cerutty became a raw vegan, took up weightlifting, read extensively in philosophy and religion, and completed a 500-mile hike along Australia's South Coast. Having run competitively in school, he returned to the sport with a new mindset and self-discovered methods, completing a marathon in 2:58:11 at age 52, the best time ever recorded by a runner of any age from the state of Victoria.

Around the same time, Cerutty purchased a beachside property in Portsea with the intent of hosting training camps for the runners he now coached. At Ceres (the name he bestowed on the property), he not only put his athletes through their paces but also indoctrinated them in a philosophy he called Stotanism, which combined elements of Stoicism and of the simple, ascetic lifestyle that is associated with the warrior society of ancient Sparta. Signing on to the program meant signing up for barefoot running, a primal diet, sleeping in bunks, daily readings in philosophy and poetry, and an overall lifestyle shorn of modern comforts, distractions, and conveniences.

Cerutty's comeback had taught him that dependence is weakness. The less we choose to need, and the less we rely on comfortable, favorable circumstances for peace of mind, the more control we have over our thoughts, emotions, and behavior. "Pain is the purifier," he taught. "Walk towards suffering. Love suffering. Embrace it."

Among those who signed on to this approach was a prodigal 18-year-old miler named Herb Elliott, who became Stotanism's greatest success story, setting world records at the one-mile and 1500-meter distances and winning the 1960 Olympic 1500 meters. "He coaches your spirit," Herb once said of his coach. "The body itself may only need two months to get fit; the rest of the time you're building up your spirit—call it guts or some inner force—so that it will go to work for you in a race without your even knowing it."

A staple of Cerutty's training was barefoot sprints up steep sand dunes, which were repeated until the runner literally dropped. Not above joining the action himself sometimes, Cerutty more often stood by observing, calling out to his suffering athletes, "Faster, *it's only pain.*" For my money, no three words better encapsulate the ultrarealist's attitude toward discomfort.

Perhaps the best contemporary example of an athlete espousing an ultrarealist philosophy is Eliud Kipchoge, whom we met briefly already. Widely regarded as the greatest marathoner ever born, Eliud has won all but one of the marathons he's entered and holds both the official (2:01:40) and unofficial (1:59:40, recorded in a special time trial) world records at this distance. He's also rich, especially by the standards of his native Kenya, but you wouldn't know it by his lifestyle.

Raised by a single mother in a small village, Eliud sold milk that he collected from neighbors at a local market to help the family make ends meet. Now a multimillionaire, he chooses to maintain a similarly hand-to-mouth lifestyle during marathon buildups. When it's time to get serious about training, Eliud leaves the home he shares with his wife and three children in the city of Eldoret and heads up the hill to the high-altitude village of Kaptagat, where he takes up residence at a Ceres-like training camp operated by his longtime coach, Patrick Sang. By choice rather than necessity, Eliud sleeps with a roommate in a tin-roofed dormitory, rises at five o'clock every morning, is running by six, and spends the rest of the day eating simple, traditional Kenyan fare such as ugali (an unseasoned cornmeal cake); resting and napping; running some more; reading books on philosophy and self-help (Confucius, Aristotle, Covey); counseling his younger training partners (who've nicknamed him "the Philosopher"); and doing chores that include cooking, gardening, and swabbing toilets.

Eliud does these things not because he likes sleeping next to a snoring teammate or scrubbing fecal residue off porcelain but rather because, like the Buddha, and Zeno of Citium, and Epictetus, and Percy Cerutty, he believes that success and happiness arise out of self-mastery, and self-mastery out of reducing external wants and wishes and needs to a bare minimum. "Only the disciplined ones are free in life," he said in a 2018 speech at England's Oxford Union. "If you aren't disciplined, you are a slave to your moods. You are a slave to your passions. That's a fact."

As with meditation, ascetic living is not a necessary tool for cultivating ultrarealism, but there's a reason ultrarealists often use it. When you give up material comforts and choose to make do with little, you are better prepared to respond effectively when things don't go your way in training or competition. Ask yourself who is more likely to take it in stride when his racing flats spontaneously fall apart during a marathon: an athlete who "needs" a television and a soft mattress or one who doesn't?

Less than six miles into the 2015 Berlin Marathon, the insoles of Eliud Kipchoge's Nikes came unglued and began to slip, and by the midpoint of the race they were dangling over the sides of the shoes like living critters fighting to escape captivity. His left foot became severely blistered, and a cut opened on the big toe. Most runners know how painful it is to jog with a hot spot, but few know how painful it is to blaze 4:45 miles with a foot bathed in its own blood. Despite the pain, Eliud appears to have executed the race exactly as he would have done otherwise, surging at 30 kilometers and dashing away to an 81-second victory against a stacked field.

"It is a good shoe, and I have tested that same shoe in training, but that is sport," he told reporters afterward. "I have to accept it. I had pain in my foot, but what could I do? I had to finish the race."

It cannot be overstated how different this reaction is from the reaction most runners would have had in the same situation. Eight out of 10, I'm willing to bet, would have thought, *I can't believe this is happening!*—words that convey a literal rejection of present reality. But as surprising, bizarre, and dismaying as Eliud's mid-race footwear malfunction must surely have been for him, he treated it as just another challenge, or perhaps more accurately, as part of the challenge he'd signed up for, and therefore no less inevitable than feeling tired in the late miles.

> *That is sport.*
> *I have to accept it.*
> *I had to finish.*

THE SCIENCE OF ULTRAREALISM

Around the same time Percy Cerutty was initiating Aussie runners into the version of ultrarealism he called Stotanism, formal exploration of ultrealism's underlying truths began to migrate from the realms of religion and philosophy into that of science. A key early figure in this process was the psychiatrist William Glasser, who in the 1960s developed a new method of psychotherapy he called reality therapy.

To athletes, Glasser is best known as the author of the 1976 book *Positive Addiction*, in which he explored commonalities between meditation and running, both of which, his research found, induce altered mind states that, for some, become addictive, but in a way that (unlike other addictions) strengthens rather than weakens the individual. In the behavioral health realm, though, Glasser's greatest legacy is reality therapy, a pragmatic approach to counseling that grew out of his disillusionment with the Freudian paradigm that dominated his field in the early part of his career.

The psychoanalytic method that Freud pioneered involves probing the patient's deep past for the root of their present complaint and is based on the belief that knowing the source of the problem will free the patient from its influence. In his own clinical experience, however, Glasser found the opposite to be true—that this method more often served only to absolve the patient of responsibility for their present behavior, hence also of the power to change it. Reality therapy, by contrast, is all about forcing the patient to take responsibility. "No reason is acceptable to the [reality] therapist for any irresponsible behavior," he wrote in his original book on the subject. "He confronts the patient with his behavior and asks him to decide whether or not he is taking the responsible course."

The theoretical underpinning of reality therapy is choice theory, another product of Glasser's fertile mind, which posits that all humans share certain basic needs, and that any and all feelings and behaviors that cause a person to seek counseling are rooted in failure to meet one of these needs, whether it be love or recognition or professional success or something else. Strong and weak people alike fail to meet their needs sometimes, but in Glasser's view, whereas the strong (mentally fit) accept responsibility for their failure and take adaptive action, the weak (mentally less fit), unable to accept the reality of their situation, resort to maladaptive actions such as withdrawal and alcohol abuse. "In their unsuccessful efforts to fulfill their needs, no matter what behavior they choose," Glasser wrote, "all patients have a common characteristic: *they all deny the reality of the world around them . . .* Therapy will be successful when they are able to give up denying the world and recognize [not only that reality] exists but that they must fulfill their needs within its framework."

It is easy to recognize this formulation as a modern complement to the Buddha's ancient wisdom. The Buddha saw suffering as stemming from the mistaken belief that our wants are actually needs. Glasser points out that it also works the other way: Our inability to fulfill our (true) needs can sometimes give rise to self-deceptions intended to disguise this painful reality. Most psychotherapeutic methods involve helping patients liberate themselves from self-deception. What makes reality therapy different is the centrality of this project to the method. Reality therapy is all about getting people to stop bullshitting themselves so they can get on with the business of solving the real problem. At no point does the reality therapist ever allow a patient to get away with denying reality, no matter how painful accepting it may be initially.

This might sound kind of mean, but in fact it's the opposite. The unofficial motto of reality therapy is "No judgment, no excuses, never give up." Reality therapists take pains to avoid making patients feel ashamed of either their self-deceptions or of the unmet needs that give rise to them. The point of forcing patients to face these realities in a nonjudgmental way is to train them to regard *all* realities as acceptable—to fear no truth. And the underlying truth in every bad situation is that, no matter what caused it, *you* are responsible for making the best of it. The sooner you can get to a point where it's no longer off-limits to look squarely at your role in your bad situation, the sooner you can cease making excuses, embrace your capacity to make your situation different rather than wishing it were different, and address it to the very best of your ability.

It has been my experience that some form of self-deception is almost always at play when an athlete is struggling to deal with a bad situation, and that no solution is possible until and unless the athlete is liberated from it. This is why I have found reality therapy (which Glasser himself insisted that anyone can practice with a little training, not just PhDs like himself) so useful in my coaching work.

Here's an example. Carla hired me to coach her after she suffered a freak health scare in her first half-marathon that left her with a diagnosed case of post-traumatic stress disorder. A psychologist had already been engaged to help her with the PTSD; my job was to train her for a second attempt at the same event that had ended so badly for her the year before—a major step in her recovery.

We'd only been working together for a few days when Carla suffered a setback that was triggered by news of an assault on a woman who had been running in an area where Carla herself frequently trained. The incident shook the entire local running community, but no one was hit harder than Carla, who found herself unable to eat or sleep and doubting her ability to finish out her week's training.

I'm no psychologist, and I've never been through anything remotely like what Carla went through in her first half-marathon, but when she told me she thought it would be wise to take a few days off, I suspected she might be deceiving herself. My hunch was that her perceived need to "process" what had happened and to get back on track with her diet and sleep before running again were excuses, and that the real issue was Carla's own fear of running, which predated the assault.

We talked through the situation in a video call. I gave Carla space to articulate her distress and validated her belief that taking a few days off might be the right course of action, because for all I knew it was. Then I asked Carla to give me a reason why she might be better off *not* pausing her training, and with a little coaxing, she voiced my own hunch in her own words. I made it clear to her that both possibilities were equally acceptable and that the decision was hers to make. The only thing I insisted on was that she make her choice with total clarity about what it represented. I could see the relief on Carla's face when she understood that my assessment of the situation came entirely without judgment. She decided to continue training, and not only that, but to do her next run at the very place where the assault had occurred (the culprit having been apprehended). It wasn't easy, but she got through it and was rightly proud of herself for doing so—and she went on to crush the race that had crushed her the first time.

I'm not trying to sell you on reality therapy any more than I was trying to sell you on mindfulness meditation. It's simply an instrument that has been useful in my efforts to help athletes face reality. Other approaches work equally well, provided they aim toward the same end.

Since reality therapy's heyday in the 1970s, the field of clinical psychology has taken an empirical turn, producing research that has scientifically validated the idea that facing reality is essential to worldly coping. Among the newer therapies backed by such research is acceptance and commitment therapy (ACT), in which patients are trained to accept negative emotions and divorce them from their source, so that the patient can avoid reacting to them reflexively and instead take a more rational line toward solving the underlying problem. The ACT acronym does double duty, serving also to describe the method's three steps, which align perfectly with the three steps ultrarealists take in making the best of a bad situation:

Accept your reactions and be present (accept reality)
Choose a valued direction (embrace reality)
Take action (address reality)

Studies have shown that ACT is effective in helping people overcome a wide range of fears, anxieties, and aversions, including aversion to the discomfort of endurance exercise. One such study was led by Elena Ivanova of McMaster University in Canada and published in *Medicine & Science in Sport*

& *Exercise* in 2015. The subjects were 39 women between the ages of 18 and 45 who were not currently involved in a regular exercise program. Part one of the experiment was a stationary bike ride to exhaustion at 80 percent of maximal power output, which lasted about six and half minutes for the average subject. Afterward, half of the subjects received a single, 40-minute lesson in acceptance and commitment therapy. The two main objectives of this lesson were "to help participants disentangle their physical sensations (e.g., burning legs) from their thoughts (e.g., 'I must stop exercising') and behaviors (e.g., quit exercising)" and "to help increase participants' willingness to experience consequences of a valued behavior (e.g., exercising) that may carry unpleasant physical sensations, without trying to change, control, or eliminate them."

The last part of the experiment was a repetition of the stationary cycling test, and you can probably guess what happened. The women who had learned acceptance and commitment techniques lasted an average of 15 percent longer than they had the first time, even though they weren't any fitter. In contrast, the control subjects performed slightly worse than before. The ACT group also reported lower levels of perceived effort during the test and higher levels of "exercise enjoyment" afterward.

Discomfort is a performance limiter not just for beginning exercisers but for competitive athletes at every level of performance, right up to the top, so it's no stretch to generalize these findings to encompass the entire athlete population. No matter where you stand on the mental fitness spectrum, accepting more fully the reality of discomfort and other negative sensations will make you feel and perform better.

AT ONE WITH THE UNIVERSE

Recent discoveries in brain science have further corroborated the Buddha's key insight. A new theory of consciousness known as predictive processing offers an intriguing explanation for why people feel and perform better when they align themselves with reality. Developed by Karl Friston, a British neuroscientist, this theory proposes that the human mind is fundamentally a prediction engine, whose primary job is to generate representations of what is likely to happen next, for the sake of guiding action in an effective way. The more accurate the mind's predictions are, the more effective the actions based upon these predictions will be and the more likely it is that the person performing them will survive and thrive in the world.

This view of consciousness is radically different from the traditional view, in which the mind was understood to be mainly reactive in its functioning. Prior to Friston, sight, hearing, and other perceptions were thought to be used to receive information about the present state of reality so that a person could respond appropriately. According to the predictive processing model, however, perception is used primarily to identify discrepancies between the reality that is expected (based on information gathered from a lifetime of past perceptions) and actual reality. These discrepancies are then used to improve future predictions.

Predictive processing theory is supported by a rapidly expanding body of neuroscience research suggesting that consciousness truly is built on expectation. For example, it has been demonstrated that the brain's reward system works in this manner—when a mismatch occurs between an anticipated reward and an actual reward, the discrepancy is encoded by dopamine neurons in a way that refines future reward predictions and guides future behavior. Predictive processing theory is not completely uncontroversial, but if this explanation of consciousness is more or less correct, it becomes a lot easier to understand why the greatest minds in religion and philosophy and psychology (and sport) keep coming back to the idea that success depends on never being thrown off by what reality tosses at you. In the old view of consciousness, everyone's picture of reality is as good as their sight and hearing, and success is a matter of choosing the best response to what the eyes and ears report. But in this new view, our eyes and ears serve mainly to test how well we know reality, and successful action depends on just how well actually we do.

Endurance racing is a paradigmatic example of predictive processing at work. An endurance race can be defined as any race of sufficient length that fatigue is the primary performance limiter, such that athletes are required to move at less-than-maximum speed to reach the finish line in minimum time. In such a race, athletes must pace themselves, holding back just enough to reach the finish line before an involuntary slowdown occurs. Effective pacing is done mostly by feel. There is no such thing as a device, test, or calculator that can tell an athlete how fast to go at every moment throughout a race to reach the finish line in the least time possible.

A perfectly paced race is one in which the athlete maintains a fairly steady speed (allowing for some variation based on topography and other conditions) the whole way and crosses the finish line feeling as though they're on the brink of hitting the wall. At the beginning of every race, perfect execution exists as a potential reality. The athlete then tries to actualize this reality through predictive processing, which in this case entails feeling their way to just the right speed, moment by moment, until the finish line is reached.

In longer events especially, this is very difficult to do, and yet some athletes get to be remarkably good at it. Consider American runner Meb Keflezighi's winning performance at the 2014 Boston Marathon. Seven miles in, Meb made a surprise move, surging away from the lead pack and building a 90-second lead over the next 11 miles. By mile 19, the chase was on, Kenyan Wilson Chebet closing to within 11 seconds of Meb on the homestretch, but that's as close as he got. The first American winner of the Boston Marathon in 31 years fulfilled both conditions of perfect pacing in this race, covering the second half just five seconds faster than the first and neither speeding up nor slowing down in the final meters despite being chased and despite being blind with exhaustion.

The late stages of a perfectly paced endurance race aren't much fun. Yet these races are immensely popular. Each year, 30,000 runners from all over the world run the Boston Marathon for the chance to finish blind with exhaustion, and hundreds of thousands of others attempt to qualify. Predictive processing theory helps us explain what attracts people to endurance racing, which in its essence is the art of pacing, a formalized way of doing what our minds exist to do: use our perceptions to predict future reality and make our actions align with it. As painful as it is, endurance racing feels oddly right to many because, in a deep sense, we were born for it.

But it goes even deeper. Karl Friston, the man who came up with the predictive processing model of consciousness, has also played a lead role in developing something known as the free energy principle, a mathematical concept that originated in physics but applies also, Friston and others believe, to the animate realm, explaining all of life. In a nutshell, the free-energy principle postulates that every living entity, from single-cell protozoa to the 100-billion-cell human brain, operates in mathematically predictable ways to minimize free energy, which is the gap between expected reality and actual reality. All of life depends on the ability of the living thing to maintain a clear distinction between inside and outside, between self and external reality, and it does this by continuously tuning itself to reality. Support for the free energy principle comes largely from virtual reality games in which artificial agents programmed to learn by minimizing prediction errors, or surprise, outperform agents programmed to learn in other ways.

WHY AREN'T WE ALL ULTRAREALISTS?

Let's review. More than 2,400 years ago, an Indian spiritual seeker discovered that the secret to happiness lay in not wishing things were different than they are. Over the centuries that followed, many other thinkers, including the Stoics of Greece, arrived at the same truth. Beginning in the 20th century, coaches and athletes realized that facing reality not only promoted happiness by eliminating wants but also enhanced one's ability to fulfill wants (such as success in competition) and needs, and psychologists including William Glasser verified their observations in clinical settings. Recent advances in neuroscience and other hard sciences suggest that the capacity of living things to read reality and align themselves with it is the key to surviving and thriving in the world. And now here I am, putting a sport-specific twist on this concept, proposing that the substance of mental fitness is a readiness to accept, embrace, and address reality just as it is, no matter how bad the situation.

If all of this is true, you might be wondering, then why do so many athletes struggle to face reality? Why aren't we all ultrarealists? Keep reading.

6½ MONTHS TO SANTA ROSA

If I didn't know it before, I know it now: It's easier to promise you won't bullshit yourself than it is to actually not bullshit yourself. Today I suffered what I fear is a significant setback with my groin, and it's all because I didn't accept a reality that was staring me in the face.

As I write these words, I'm sitting at a desk in my father's home office in North Kingstown, Rhode Island, enjoying an oblique view of Narragansett Bay. I've been visiting my folks often—about once every eight weeks—since my mother was diagnosed with Alzheimer's disease last year, and I have no intention of allowing my triathlon comeback to subvert this commitment. In this respect, so far, I am doing as I believe an ultrarealist would do in my position. Instead of worrying about how I'm going to stay consistent with my training if I keep flying across the country so frequently, I am simply challenging myself to find a way.

As it happens, my older brother, Josh, is here now too, having travelled separately from Salem, Oregon. He and I have a long history of running together, and one of the reasons we timed our visits to overlap was a shared desire to run together in a place where he and I have logged hundreds of happy miles over the decades. The eagerness with which I looked forward to this renewal of our fraternal training-partner relationship was, I see in hindsight, the seed of the judgment error that put me where I am now.

Prior to today I was very careful. Spooked by a setback in August, eight weeks into my Ironman quest, I stopped running for four weeks, determined to snuff out the inflammation once and for all, substituting uphill treadmill walks for the runs I wasn't doing in the meantime. After that I went through a cautious process of returning to normal run training, which went smoothly. I completed 12 slow, pain-free miles on September 29, 14 miles on October 7, and 16 miles six days later.

The plan this morning was to run 18 miles, the first 8 alone, the last 10 with Josh. I set out conservatively, covering the first mile in 7:43, and then let my body dictate the pace. Fitness-wise I felt good, stronger than at any earlier point since I started running again, and my groin was quiet, so I found myself gradually accelerating as I continued.

Midway through a 7:17 seventh mile, I felt a sudden twinge. It was nothing like the nail-gun shot I experienced when the initial injury occurred 14 months ago, but it left behind a worrisome soreness, and throughout the remaining 1.5 miles of the solo portion of the run I went back and forth in my mind about whether to go ahead with the plan of finishing with my brother or bail out instead. I knew that bailing out was the prudent thing to do, but I hated the thought of missing out on running with Josh—not to mention missing out on those 10 miles.

In the end, emotion won out over reason, and I continued. Josh requested a slower pace, which I was all for given the circumstances, but even at 8:15 per mile, my groin remained sore for the balance of the run, and now, 24 hours later, I feel it even when I walk, so there can be no doubt that I'm looking at yet another extended layoff from running.

It is unlikely that an ultrarealist would have made such an obvious mistake. Having made it, I can only look ahead, asking myself: What would an ultrarealist do now? My guess is that they would vow never to make the same mistake again, no matter the temptation, so that's what I've done. An ultrarealist in my shoes would also keep perspective, I believe, so I'm doing that also. Indeed things could be worse. Overcoming this injury is almost entirely within my control. All I have to do is stay patient and disciplined—not *most* of the way through the recovery process this time but *all* the way.

This commitment, and the clarity of vision that supports it, has helped me relax a little. It sucks that I sabotaged myself once again, and it also sucks that I can't run for a while, but I'm embracing the challenge of proving that I can get all the way back to 100 percent without any reliance on factors beyond my control. Would I have this mindset if I weren't consciously following the Ultrarealist's Creed in this journey? I doubt it. Clearly, adopting the creed hasn't stopped me from making the kind of mistake that has been all too typical of me in my athletic career, and in this sense, the experiment I've undertaken hasn't entirely succeeded to this point. On the other hand, in consideration of how I'm handling the misstep, I think it's equally true that it hasn't entirely failed, either.

3

ACCEPTING REALITY

Whatever the present moment contains, accept it as if you had chosen it.
ECKHART TOLLE

PETRA MAJDIČ ARRIVED in Vancouver, British Columbia, for the 2010 Winter Olympics in top form. Considered a gold-medal contender in the women's sprint event, the 30-year-old Slovenian cross-country skier had racked up six podium finishes, including three wins, in eight World Cup events leading up to the Games. On the morning of day five, Petra was transported from the Olympic Village to nearby Whistler Olympic Park to prepare for the day's racing, which for her would consist of four rounds of sprint races (assuming she kept advancing) in the span of four hours. In her practice starts, she outpaced several male competitors as her coach, Ivan Hudač, looked on, struggling to maintain a poker face. She was so ready.

Then disaster struck. While cruising around the 1.4 km course minutes before the start of the qualifying round, Petra lost control on an icy corner and skidded into a 10-foot-deep gully, landing in a rocky creek bed. A blast of pain in Petra's back sent a reflexive cry back to the surface she had just vanished from, drawing a rush of would-be rescuers to the crater's edge. Instead of waiting for rescue, however, Petra gathered her wits and scaled up the snowy precipice, the whole right side of her torso ablaze, repeating the same words over and over to the stricken race officials who received her at the top: "Take me to the starting line!"

In a later interview, Petra explained that "too much had gone into that moment" for her to even consider not racing. Nearly her entire life, in fact, had gone into that moment. Raised on a farm in Kamnik, a small town in the Slovenian Alps, Petra had few advantages as far as her athletic ambitions were concerned. For starters, Slovenia had never produced an Olympic medalist in cross-country skiing, offering scandalously little developmental support to aspiring young skiers for a country with so much snow. At home, Petra got even less support from her parents, who regarded her skiing as a frivolous waste of time and a distraction from the rigorous daily farm work they required of her and her two brothers. "Don Quixote," her mother called her, a teasing reference to the delusional fictional battler of imagined giants. But Petra showed enough early promise and more than enough stubbornness of will that her first coach, Robert Slabanja, was eventually able to talk her folks into releasing her from farm duties, sharing Petra's conviction that her athletic dreams were far from delusional.

Petra made her World Cup debut in 1999, recorded her first point (i.e., top-30 placing) a year later, reached the podium a year after that, and made her first Olympic appearance in Salt Lake City in 2002. But further progress was rendered frustratingly difficult by her straitened circumstances—inferior equipment, second-rate training conditions, self-funded travel. Recognizing that only by succeeding despite her disadvantages could she earn a more level playing field, Petra worked her tail off until, in 2006, she scored a long-sought World Cup win and with it a sinecure with the Slovenian armed forces, a new coach, and a full-service support team.

At the 2006 Olympics in Turin, Petra was in a lead group of 11 racers in the 10 km classic event when a crewman for the German team bumbled onto the course and collided with her, knocking her to the ground. She rebounded to finish sixth, but Petra would have to wait four long years for her next—and probably last—chance to win her country's first Olympic medal in cross-country skiing.

Then the accident in Whistler. It wasn't just Petra's body that sustained major damage in her plunge into the gully. She also broke a ski and both poles. Mercifully, race officials allowed her to move to the back of the qualifying round of the sprint, a time trial in which athletes were sent off at 30-second intervals to compete against the clock. In principle, this gave Petra time to find new gear and regroup, but in reality, her undiagnosed injuries hurt so much that she could neither sit nor move as she awaited her turn, and she began to wish she could just get on with it. When her number finally came up, Coach Hudač, who had tried to talk Petra out of racing, urged her to coast the loop, doing just enough to say she hadn't quit, and then go to the hospital, but she had other ideas. "I didn't think any more about the medal," she recalled in an interview for the Olympic Channel. "It was just about not [giving] up. It was just about trying."

Petra's mincing approach to the start line evoked gasps of disbelief from her fellow racers and their coaches, word of her accident having spread quickly. The beginning of the race was like a leap from a great height, a blind dive into a depth of agony Petra could never have imagined. An involuntary shriek of raw torment escaped her with every exhalation, clusters of concerned spectators falling silent as she poled her way around the circuit. On crossing the finish line, Petra fell to the ground and curled into a ball, moaning piteously. But the work was done. Needing a top-30 time to advance to the quarterfinal, she got 19th.

She had 75 minutes to gird herself for the next sufferfest, most of which time she spent on an examination table at an onsite mobile medical unit. The tiny facility lacked X-ray capability, so a less-reliable ultrasound machine was used to check for fractured ribs. None were found, and Petra was cleared to race. She needed help just getting off the table. It was absurd.

Having refused an analgesic injection at the clinic out of fear that it might harm her performance, Petra decided not to bother warming up for the quarterfinal, rationing her pain tolerance. In the minutes before the race, team psychologist Matej Tušak decided to try something.

"Do you have pain in your arms?" he asked.

"No," Petra said.

"Do you have pain in your legs?"

Same answer.

"Then concentrate only on your arms and legs," he suggested.

It was weak medicine. Again Petra screamed her way around the course and again she collapsed at the finish, yet somehow she'd won her quarterfinal and qualified for the semis. The pain was getting worse, however, and during the two-hour wait for her next race, Petra told Hudač she'd had enough. Expecting grateful acquiescence, she was stunned when instead her coach berated her, letting loose an utterly out-of-character display of temper.

This, too, was Tušak's idea. Hudač had approached him earlier and asked what he could do to help Petra. The psychologist suggested Hudač yell at her, as this would make her angry and thus cause her adrenal glands to release pain-masking epinephrine into her bloodstream. It was all they had.

Midway through the semifinal, there was a second explosion, deep in Petra's right side. It felt as though a knife had pierced her lung and been left there to saw at her insides as she continued to grind toward the finish. She needed to place first or second to gain automatic advancement to the final, but she fell off the pace and crossed the line fourth. Petra had done enough, however, to secure the second of two "lucky loser" slots awarded to the fastest nonautomatic qualifiers. By the skin of her teeth, she'd earned herself one last sufferfest.

At 1:45 that afternoon, four hours after her accident, Petra joined five other women on the start line for the women's sprint final. She was realistic. Marit Bjørgen of Norway and Justyna Kowalczyk of Poland were beyond her reach in her current condition. But bronze seemed attainable. To claim it, she would have to overcome not only otherworldly pain but also crushing fatigue—more than the usual amount of fatigue after three rounds of racing.

During the first half of the race, Petra remained mired in fourth place behind Sweden's Anna Olsson, struggling to control her tired body, veering wide on a sharp bend and nearly sailing off course a second time. With 400 meters to go and time running out, Petra chose to glide a second or two longer than the others on the last descent, needing that extra bit of rest. She then poled with everything she had, lungs shrieking, telling herself, *You can get it. You can get it.* And she got it, the tips of Petra's skis breaching the line 0.7 second ahead of Anna's. Petra raised her arms in weary celebration and then dropped to the snow, where she lay semiconscious and hyperventilating, shaking her head at the water bottle that was put to her lips by a medic. Eventually she was carried away, limp as a squid. But she had her medal— *a* medal, at least.

BARRIERS TO ACCEPTING REALITY

Sometimes defeat is inescapable. When it is, an athlete may either accept their defeat or be resigned to it. They're not the same thing. Both involve admitting defeat. But there are two different ways of interpreting a defeat you've admitted. One is to wish it hadn't happened—to admit it without really accepting it, in other words. That's resignation. The other is to pivot from wishing the defeat hadn't happened to trying to make the best of it.

Recall from Chapter 1 that accepting a bad situation entails perceiving it in a way that preserves your ability to make choices. An athlete who accepts defeat instead of merely being resigned to it looks for ways to make something of it, perhaps by using it as an opportunity for learning and growth, or possibly by transforming it into a stepping-stone toward ultimate victory in reframing it as just one chapter of a larger story. Petra Majdič was defeated in her bid for gold in Vancouver before her first race even started, but she made the best of it by recasting her participation in the sprints as a "never-quit story," as she has called it. Few athletes in Petra's position would have found the wherewithal to move on from wishing their defeat hadn't happened to trying to make something of it as quickly and completely as she did. Why do athletes so often fail to accept the reality of a bad situation?

Because accepting reality is hard, that's why! It's like lifting a heavy object off the ground; the most effective way to do so is to squat down and use the legs, but in the absence of proper instruction, many people bend from the waist and use the upper body because it requires a smaller initial energy investment, and it is the nature of all creatures to take perceived shortcuts even when the long way is actually faster. Similarly, each of us possesses certain instincts that dispose us to take a seemingly easier path in situations where accepting reality is threatening or is deemed more trouble than it's worth. There are three such instincts in particular that commonly prevent athletes from accepting the reality of a bad situation:

1) Fear and laziness: turning away from scary or daunting realities
2) Cognitive bias: blindness to realities that undermine our beliefs
3) Ego defense: tuning out realities that threaten our self-image

Let's take a closer look at each of these instincts and explore how ultra-realists override them.

Fear and Laziness

The next time you go to the theater to watch a scary movie, wait for the part where the main character is creeping through a darkened house, spooked by creaking sounds, pulling back shower curtains and peering into closets, and you know a monster attack is coming, but you don't know when or how it's going to go down, and then take a moment to look around at your fellow moviegoers. At least a few of them will have shut or shielded their eyes. Indeed, chances are good you've done exactly the same thing when watching scary movies.

Looking away from scary things is normal human behavior. We do it to protect ourselves from fear itself and from painful realities. Monsters aren't real, of course, but plenty of other things, such as bereavement, are all too real. Denial is a famously common symptom of grief, for example. In her book *Shattered Assumptions: Towards a New Psychology of Trauma*, psychologist Ronnie Janoff-Bulman argues that temporarily blocking the truth of a loved one's death or some other traumatic event is a natural way for grieving individuals to prepare themselves to accept what they will eventually have to accept.

Milder forms of turning away from daunting realities occur all the time in everyday life. Among the most common is what I call sour grapes syndrome: pretending you don't want what you can't have. In Aesop's fable about the fox and the grapes, a fox is walking along in the forest when he spots a juicy bunch of grapes hanging from a branch. He leaps upward and tries to snatch them between his teeth but he misses. He tries a second time and misses again. After a third miss he gives up and slinks away, muttering, "They're probably sour anyway."

Sour grapes syndrome is common among endurance athletes at all levels. Some athletes who take up cycling or running or triathlon as adults do not react well to the discovery that they're not as competitive as they would like to be. Some choose to deal with their disappointment by redefining "winning" in a way that makes them winners. One way they do so is by adopting alternative practices such as barefoot running, CrossFit, and ketogenic diets that are not widely used by the most competitive athletes. Then they go on social media to advocate for these practices and chide athletes who use mainstream methods for their benightedness.

Higher echelons of athletes are not immune from sour grapes syndrome. A few years ago, when the Boston Athletic Association stiffened qualifying standards for the Boston Marathon, many runners who had desperately wanted to qualify but who now felt they had almost no chance of making the cut declared that the whole obsession with BQ'ing was an elitist trap that was ruining the sport. Elite athletes do something similar when they whisper of a rival who's beaten them, "I'll bet they're on drugs."

Other ways of allowing fear or laziness to stand in the way of accepting reality are more insidious. Many triathletes rationalize the mistake of spending the least amount of time training in their weakest discipline by convincing themselves that their time is better spent further strengthening their strongest discipline. This is seldom actually true, and on some level most athletes know it, but the prospect of putting more time and effort into their least favorite discipline (and a triathlete's weakest discipline is almost always also their least favorite) is just too daunting to accept.

Diet is an area where athletes (like nonathletes) deny reality in all kinds of ways. Research has shown that an individual's unwillingness to make healthy diet changes is linked to the belief that making such changes won't bring about desired results. A study conducted at the University of Kentucky School of Nursing and published in *The Journal of Cardiac Failure* in 2012, for example, found a strong correlation between the perceived benefits of adhering to a low-sodium diet and actual long-term adherence in a population of 74 patients with heart failure. The truth, of course, is that healthy diet changes yield positive results for everyone. Making healthier eating habits stick isn't easy, however, and some people choose to believe they are an exception to the rule to avoid having to admit to themselves that they simply don't want to give up their beloved fast-food burgers.

Alison, a runner I used to coach whose diet left a lot of room for improvement, told me that she once tried eating better, but she felt awful, and her running suffered, so she went back to what "worked" for her (lots of sweets and not a lot of vegetables). Without dismissing the validity of her experience, I assured Alison that if she tried again with my help, making sensible improvements that are known to work for *everyone*, her running would surely benefit in one way or another—whether it be through increased energy, fewer injuries, or something else. But I couldn't persuade her.

Self-awareness plays a key role in stopping fear and laziness from standing in the way of accepting a reality that must be accepted in order to make the best of a bad situation. Many organizations, particularly governments and newspapers, employ an ombudsman whose job it is to handle complaints against the organization, not in a self-protective way but rather in a way that enhances organizational self-awareness and ensures necessary corrections are made. Ultrarealists have an internal ombudsman that serves essentially the same function for them, calling bullshit when they try to deny reality. We all have those moments when our mind seems to be operating on two levels at once. On one level, we're getting sucked into making a mistake, but at the same time, on a second level, we're watching ourselves getting sucked in and shouting from one side of our brain to the other, "What the hell are you doing?"

Psychologists call this metacognition, and it's a mind state that some people experience more than others do, and ultrarealists more than anyone. It protects against failure to accept reality in much the same way good coaches protect their athletes against various forms of unwitting self-sabotage: by offering a separate perspective.

Nobody is born with a strong internal ombudsman. (According to psychologists, the average person becomes capable of metacognition around age 8.) To get good at keeping an eye on yourself, you have to work at it doggedly over a long period of time. The goal is not to exist in a permanent metacognitive state but simply to learn to take a mental step back from yourself whenever you experience fear, discouragement, or another negative emotion. At such moments there is almost always an important choice to be made, and keeping an eye on yourself allows you to see your options more clearly and make the choice that is most in line with your true values. Success in this endeavor depends heavily on how quickly you are able to awaken your internal ombudsman once you are presented with a reality that, instinctively, you don't want to accept.

But wait: Isn't lack of self-awareness itself a barrier to self-awareness? Yes. For this reason, metacognition is difficult to cultivate through good intentions alone. I keep saying I'm not trying to sell you on meditation, but it so happens that mindfulness meditation is an effective way to cultivate metacognition. This is because mindfulness meditation entails hitting the pause button on all thought, reducing consciousness to raw perception, an effort that requires the mind to, in effect, post a sentry whose duty is to keep watch and sound the alarm when the inevitable reversion from raw perception to the usual mental chatter occurs. By gaining practice in catching themselves in these slips, meditators develop a robust general capacity to step back from their own thoughts and emotions, evaluate them, and in certain cases, peg them as self-deceptions of one kind or another.

Reflective exercises are another proven cultivator of metacognitive abilities. These can take a variety of forms; for athletes, training logs offer an ideal medium. Use some space in your log to say a few words about your current top-of-mind training-related worry (or worries). Try to adopt an outside perspective on them, challenging your present assumptions and probing for potential blind spots. Bill Rodgers did an excellent job of this during his storied career as a marathon runner in the 1970s and '80s. On March 15, 1974, for example, at a time when Bill was struggling to balance 120-mile training weeks with marriage, graduate school, and low-paying work as a hospital aide, he noted, "Still have a cold and am run-down but plan to race Sunday. Am doing too much now so results of all races will probably be poor—until I learn to be more dedicated to running and do what I want to do, I will screw myself over for what????" Bill finished a disappointing 14th in the Boston Marathon a few weeks later, but the following year, more focused, he won in record time, and he had his internal ombudsman (operating through his training log) to thank for it, at least to some degree. "I think it's smart to constantly evaluate our physical feelings," Bill told me recently via email, noting that in '75 he used his training log to keep himself honest about the state of a nagging quad injury.

I don't mean to suggest that every athlete must always do what's best for their performance. All I'm saying is that, as a matter of habit, athletes should put themselves in a position where they are able to make a clear-eyed decision about how to respond whenever an obstacle to better performance presents itself. Attaining this position requires accepting reality, and accepting reality requires an active internal ombudsman. What you choose to do with your self-awareness is up to you, and it doesn't have to be what Bill Rodgers chose. To return to an earlier example, perhaps you really would rather continue to eat somewhat unhealthily and deal with the consequences than muster the discipline required to improve your diet and enjoy the benefits. That's fine; just don't lie to yourself, pretending there are no consequences.

Cognitive Bias

Up to this point I have written as if all athletes are equally capable of *seeing* reality and differ only in their willingness to *accept* the reality seen. But this is not really the case. Independent of acceptance, some athletes are better than others at perceiving reality (or certain realities) in an objective way, and even the most clear-eyed athletes struggle to perceive reality without bias at times. And you can't accept a reality you don't see.

The term *cognitive bias* is used by psychologists to denote the various ways in which people systematically misread reality in their minds. The good news is that anyone can learn to mitigate their personal cognitive biases and get better at thinking objectively. As an athlete, you'll find the effort required to achieve this improvement well worth making because it will help you put reason in the driver's seat when defining problems and identifying solutions. But understand that no small effort will be required because our minds aren't really designed for objective thinking.

As we saw in the preceding chapter, the main job of the human brain is to make predictions about the world. To perform its job effectively, the brain must first make the world predictable. This task involves creating models of reality (i.e., beliefs), a process that begins with our five senses, which are specially attuned to notice patterns. Our eyes, ears, nose, tongue, and skin function not as receptors so much as filters, tuning out some stimuli while focusing on others. "The brain is a belief engine," writes psychologist Michael Shermer in *The Believing Brain*. "From sensory data flowing in through the senses the brain naturally begins to look for and find patterns with meaning." Having identified a meaningful pattern, the brain can then make good predictions. For example: *The dog barked when the letter carrier pushed the mail through the mail slot on Monday, Tuesday, Wednesday, and Thursday. Therefore, the dog will probably do the same on Friday.*

It should be noted that efficiency is as important as accuracy in the formation of beliefs. For this reason, the brain often establishes beliefs on very limited information, and having formed these beliefs, becomes resistant to altering them in the face of new and contradictory information. "Once beliefs are formed," Shermer writes, "the brain begins to look for and find confirmatory evidence in support of those beliefs, which adds an emotional boost of further confidence in the beliefs and thereby accelerates the process of reinforcing them, and round and round the process goes in a positive feedback loop of belief confirmation." This can happen even on a cultural level, as it did in the case of the national inferiority complex that held back so many Slovenian athletes before Petra Majdič, and may have held her back early in her career ("I was just a young girl and unsure of my abilities," she once said of this period), before she decided to make it her mission to challenge this self-limiting bias through her personal example.

Getting by in the world demands not only that our beliefs be true but also that they be useful. In order to be useful, our beliefs must reflect reality to a certain degree. They need not be absolutely true, however, because it takes a lot more work to arrive at absolutely true beliefs than it does to arrive at good-enough beliefs. But what if your goal is to do more than just get by in the world?

Take scientists, for example. Their entire raison d'être is to discover absolute truth. To combat the natural human tendency to settle for good-enough truths, these seekers of knowledge developed the scientific method, which functions as a bulwark against cognitive bias, elevating belief formation into a rule-bound, collective endeavor that, when it works properly, yields models of reality that are generally more accurate than those that come about when people simply believe what it suits them to believe.

Elite athletes, too, seek to do more than just get by in the world. Members of this rarefied group aim to be nothing less than the best in the world at their sport. To succeed, they need to know and do the things that work most effectively to prepare them for competition. And to identify these methods, they must be as objective as possible in choosing from among the various options. For the most part, this is simply a matter of emulating the methods used by current and recent champions, which are the product of generations of collective high-stakes trial and error, an evolutionary process that only the "fittest" methods have survived. These methods have raised the level of competition in all major sports so high that it is no longer possible for even the most gifted individuals to succeed by choosing training, nutrition, and other methods based on a mere personal affinity for them, or out of sheer convenience.

Recreational athletes have far less at stake than the elites do. Our very livelihood does not, as theirs does, depend on knowing and doing the things that work most effectively to prepare for competition. We can often achieve a satisfactory level of success with beliefs about how to train and eat that are merely good enough. Many of us *think* we want to prepare in the most effective ways, but in the absence of the win-or-starve stakes that the pros live by, it's all too easy to fall into the trap of cognitive bias and mistake methods that are merely appealing to or convenient for us for the best methods.

I'll give you an example. A veritable mountain of scientific research has demonstrated that endurance athletes of all ability and experience levels perform best in longer races when they consume carbohydrate at a rate of at least 60 grams per hour. This fueling protocol is a proven best practice in endurance racing, indispensable to the optimization of competitive performance, and for this reason nearly all world-class endurance athletes adhere to it. But it's not always easy. The human body wasn't really designed to take in *any* nutrition during exercise, and for this reason, trying to take in 60 or more grams of carbs per hour during races (particularly running events) can be uncomfortable and may even cause severe gastrointestinal distress. This is as true for the pros as it is for non-elites, but when elite athletes encounter initial difficulty in executing this best practice, they don't just give up. Instead they persist, trying different types of drinks and gels and different ways of training their gut to tolerate what's being asked of it until they succeed, because again, their very livelihood depends on it.

Haile Gebrselassie is one such athlete. After a brilliant career on the track in the late 1990s and early 2000s, the legendary Ethiopian runner moved up to the marathon, where he struggled at first, winning only once in his first three tries at 26.2 miles and falling short of his time goals. Realizing that his inability to tolerate large amounts of fluid and carbohydrate intake was holding him back, Haile sought the help of world-renowned endurance sports nutrition researcher Asker Jeukendrup of the University of Birmingham, who placed his new star client on a program of graded exposure to nutrition in training. By taking in gradually increasing amounts of fuel during workouts, Geb was able to nudge his tolerance upward incrementally over time. In his next big race, the 2007 Berlin Marathon, Geb consumed two full liters of sports drink and water and six carbohydrate gels without major discomfort, and he broke the world record.

Haile Gebrselassie is living proof that virtually any endurance athlete can successfully fuel their races in the most effective way possible if they refuse to accept failure as an option. True, not everyone has access to Asker Jeukendrup, but this stuff isn't rocket science—the information is out there for everyone to take advantage of. Yet only a fraction of non-elite athletes actually bother. Some at least make the effort to learn the evidence-based best practices in race fueling and give them a try, only to abandon them after experiencing initial GI discomfort, deciding (often wrongly) that their body just can't handle that much carbohydrate. Others avoid the elite approach to race fueling based on a belief that carbs are unhealthy, forgetting how healthy most elite endurance athletes are. And still others never even consider fueling like the pros, but instead just copy the substandard race fueling practice of their peers, failing to consider the fact that just because something you do seems to work doesn't mean something else wouldn't work better. A 2014 study conducted by researchers at Denmark's Aalborg University found that runners instructed to consume 60 grams of carbs per hour during the Copenhagen Marathon finished the race nearly 11 minutes faster, on average, than fitness-matched peers who just did whatever they normally do (which resulted in 38 percent less carb intake).

The same pattern can be seen in general diet, training, and recovery, all of which are areas in which elite athletes adhere to best practices and most non-elites do something else. It's not that the pros are smarter than the rest of us. They just have the advantage of the win-or-starve stakes of elite-level competition, which function as a corrective against the natural human tendency to form good-enough beliefs that do not reflect reality with perfect accuracy.

I get it—not every athlete has access to the resources that enable the pros to follow best practices. But as I said before, the underlying information is out there, accessible to everyone. My advice for recreational athletes who wish not to be limited unnecessarily by cognitive bias is to play the "What would a pro do?" game. Pretend you will literally lose your job if you don't find and adopt the most effective methods of preparing for races, and then go about the process in the same way the pros do, which is by learning the science and emulating the medal winners. I'm not talking about blind copycatting. For example, if you're a runner, emulating the elite best training practice of training at very high volumes does not mean you run 120 miles per week just because elite runners do. That specific number is not the best practice. The true best practice is doing the maximally beneficial amount of running for the individual. It just so happens that this equates to about 120 miles per week for most elite runners; for you it might be half that.

The exercise of imagining yourself as an elite athlete is useful not only when you're deciding how to train and what to eat but also when you're making any important decision as an athlete, such as when and how often to race. Over-racing is one of the most common and costly mistakes I see among recreational endurance athletes. Racing is highly disruptive to the training process, and it's training, not racing, that yields improvement. Elite endurance athletes (especially those specializing in longer events) race sparingly because they know they will perform best if they don't race too often, and they know they'll be looking for work if they don't perform at their best when they do race. Recreational endurance athletes are often able to convince themselves that racing frequently isn't holding them back because they like racing and are therefore biased toward the belief that it's not harmful, and also because they are still able to make some progress in their athletic development despite over-racing, which enables cognitive bias to kick in.

Asking yourself what a pro would do in your place at each important decision point will help you overcome the natural mental biases that prevent all of us from perceiving reality accurately sometimes. I'm not saying that you always *have to* do what a professional athlete would do in your place. If, for example, you enjoy racing frequently so much that you don't mind its negative effects on your performance, so be it. But you should never decide one way or the other only because you're not seeing reality clearly.

Ego Defense

There are some realities that are hard to accept not because they threaten us from the outside but because they expose a part of ourselves we'd rather not see. The protective reflex that tempts us to turn away from these realities is not much different from the reflex that makes us startle at the sight of a snake slithering across the trail ahead. We flee physical threats because we are instinctively driven to preserve our lives. We flee from threats to our self-image because we are instinctively driven to preserve our sense that we are *worthy* of life. In Freudian psychology, this phenomenon is called ego defense.

Sour grapes syndrome is a form of ego defense. Athletes who try to redefine winning in terms of methodological purity do so because they can't bear to see themselves as being not very good at their sport. Sad as it is, sour grapes syndrome is understandable in the sense that lack of talent is a shortcoming that can't be changed (and is therefore not really a shortcoming). But other internal shortcomings that are revealed to athletes through the struggles they face *can* be changed, and in these cases it's all the more important that athletes accept them.

In one of my earlier books I shared the story of Rome Delasalas, a runner who struggled for years to accept the truth that he was afraid of success. Rome's dream was to qualify for and run the Boston Marathon, and though he had the necessary ability, he kept falling short, a victim of self-sabotage that ranged in form from smoking cigarettes to overeating. Only after Rome did some soul-searching and accepted the reality that the true cause of his failures was not these various excuses for falling short but his persistent efforts to create excuses to fall short did he get his act together and qualify for Boston.

I repeat Rome's story here because it exemplifies both the costs of rejecting reality for the sake of protecting one's ego and the benefits of overcoming this reflex. Accepting reality is *always* the best path forward in sport and life, even when the reality you accept forces you to admit you have a weakness that you need to work on. It's painful, yes, but only in the short term. In the long run, the pain of discovering you are not yet the man or woman you want to be is minuscule compared to the low-grade ongoing dissatisfaction of persisting in a delusion.

The term *self-criticism* carries negative associations in our culture. It shouldn't. True self-criticism is simply a matter of holding oneself to high standards of character and conduct. The reason we think of self-criticism as bad is that we conflate it with low self-esteem, which is a completely different animal. Low self-esteem comes from caring too much what other people think about you. The self-directed criticism involved in low self-esteem ("I'm not pretty enough," "I'm not fast enough," "I'm not skinny enough," "I'm not rich enough," "I'm not successful enough") is not true self-criticism at all but rather an internalized echo of perceived outside criticism. Low self-esteem, in other words, comes from judging yourself by the world's standards, whereas self-criticism comes from judging yourself by your own standards.

Caring too much about what other people think of you is a trap, not only because it makes your happiness dependent on things you can't control but also because the world's standards are pretty shallow. If you live for the world's approval, you'll find yourself worrying over how your car stacks up against your neighbors' cars and how many likes your last social media post got and a lot of other things that don't matter instead of focusing on important things like whether you're having a positive impact on the people around you. It can be challenging, though, to stop caring too much about what others think. As Emerson put it in "Self-Reliance," "It is easy in the world to live after the world's opinion; it is easy in solitude to live after our own; but the great man is he who in the midst of the crowd keeps with perfect sweetness the independence of solitude."

If I could offer just one revision to these otherwise perfectly wrought phrases, I would replace "great man" with "ultrarealist." Athletes capable of making the very best of the very worst situations live after their own opinion, not the world's, because as Rome Delasalas discovered, it's the only way to reach your full potential. In her autobiography, Joan Benoit, whose ultrarealist bona fides we established in Chapter 1, shared the following reflection, which exemplifies perfectly the mindset I'm talking about: "I would squirm under compliments most of the time, not in false modesty, but because I had a voice inside that said, 'Watch it.' The voice kept me ever aware of the fact that I wasn't reaching my potential."

The world's opinion can creep into an athlete's mind in subtle ways. Petra Majdič was known as a bit of a choker through much of her career. Dominant on the World Cup circuit, she tended to underperform in championship events, falling victim to self-doubts that were probably to some degree an internalization of the world's low expectations for Slovenian athletes. Her fortunes began to change when she gradually trained herself to let the inner voice representing the real Petra—the woman she wanted to be rather than the one the world expected her to be—to have the last word. When she landed in the bottom of the gully at Whistler Olympic Park, her first thought was, *It's over*. But then, "The second part of me said, I will go to the start," Petra recounted in an *Earth Times* interview. Let that "second part" of you—the one not tainted by the world's opinion—decide what happens next when you land in a gully.

IT DOESN'T MATTER

From the finish line at Whistler Olympic Park, Petra Majdič was rushed to a larger and better-equipped polyclinic, where she received a chest CT scan that revealed five broken ribs (incurred in her fall) and a punctured lung (suffered during her semifinal race). The treating physician recommended an immediate chest drainage procedure, but Petra demurred, determined to get to BC Place Stadium in downtown Vancouver in time for that evening's medal ceremony.

"No, that's impossible," she was told.

"How long does this operation take?" Petra asked.

"Fifteen minutes."

"I'll give you ten."

Petra left the hospital in a wheelchair. Wishing to avoid the theatrics of rolling onstage, yet unable to walk unassisted, she was helped onto the podium by a pair of officials, and there she received the first Olympic medal ever awarded to a Slovenian cross-country skier. In a video interview with NBC Sports, Petra explained the reason she wanted so badly to be seen on that stage, and it had everything to do with the theme of this chapter.

"I felt that for Slovenians," she said, "there was a message to be told: That it's possible. You just have to fight. It will not be easy. But you can manage. Because life is giving you as much pain as you are capable [of living] with. And on the end of that path, the goal will be reachable. You will have suffered to do [it], but it doesn't matter."

I can think of no better words to encapsulate what it means to accept the reality of a difficult situation. *It will not be easy. You will suffer. But it doesn't matter.*

6 MONTHS TO SANTA ROSA

I spent the entire morning—five hours all told—at an athlete-focused physical therapy clinic in Palo Alto, California. That's how long it takes to go through the facility's Performance Optimization Program (POP) for triathletes. There are PT clinics much closer to home, but none nearly as well suited to my needs. Meghan, the physical therapist assigned to me, not only has a master's degree in PT, but is also a certified strength and conditioning specialist, a triathlon coach, and a pretty good triathlete herself. We first met at a speaking event I did a couple of years ago, and when she heard about my triathlon comeback, she reached out to invite me in for a POP. I'd been planning to see a PT anyway, so it was a no-brainer from my perspective.

We began with a functional movement assessment. I've been subjected to this type of thing before, and the process never fails to make me feel like a mutant—weak here, tight there, unbalanced, misaligned, an all-around hopeless case. Meghan guided me through a sequence of tests designed to diagnose these defects, with special emphasis on my left hip abductors (the area I reaggravated recently while running with my brother), my right knee (the one that becomes painful whenever I start logging serious bike miles, as I've been doing the past three months), and my right shoulder, which has throbbed lately during swims.

When the assessment was complete, Meghan showed me a series of exercises intended to correct the limitations in strength, flexibility, and mobility that are likely contributing to my aches and pains. Some of them are rather exotic—so much so that Meghan used my cellphone to record videos of me doing them for future reference. A handful of the exercises will require me to purchase special equipment, including a pair of slide disks that I will use to do an exercise for the hip abductors that entails imitating a skating motion.

The most hopeful discovery Meghan made was a bunch of tissue damage running the entire length of my left inner thigh that I wasn't even aware of because it doesn't hurt when I run. She encouraged me to massage the area every day with a foam roller and a lacrosse ball in order to loosen up the tissue and take some strain off my injured groin tendon. The full routine that she prescribed is going to be quite time-consuming, but I promised her I'd do it religiously, and I will. I'm approaching my comeback as though my very liveli-hood depends on my success, and I know that professional triathletes, whose livelihood actually does depend on racing success, are model PT patients.

Next, we drove to a nearby pool that Meghan uses to conduct swim stroke analysis. I warmed up and then swam half a dozen laps at roughly Ironman race effort while Meghan filmed me underwater. Back at the clinic, she took me through the footage in slo-mo, adding markups at key points.

I was braced for a brutal critique of my stroke, and that's what I got. Among the flaws Meghan identified were failing to extend my lead arm sufficiently in the glide phase, dropping my elbow in the pull phase, pulling too wide with my left arm, looking too far ahead in the water, and holding my ankles too rigid, which makes my kick anti-propulsive. The nice thing about hearing all of this from a PT was that, unlike a regular swim coach, Meghan didn't blame every-thing on technique. For example, she explained that addressing tightness in my chest muscles and mobility limitations in my shoulders should help me get better shoulder extension.

After a lunch break, I got a bike fitting from the clinic's resident bike fitter, Justin. I don't have a triathlon bike yet because I wanted to get a fitting done first in case the results precluded certain brands and models. In addition to dialing in my ideal setup, Justin analyzed my pedal stroke to see what might be causing my knee pain. His conclusion was that adding special orthotic insoles to my bike shoes might help, and he handed me a pair in my size. Per-haps it was a placebo effect, but I felt a difference immediately.

My last stop of the day was the treadmill, where Meghan filmed and ana-lyzed my running stride. I've had this done before too, and the usual abnormal-ities were highlighted: asymmetrical spine rotation, lateral pelvic hip drop, inadequate rear hip extension. Clearly the exercises I've already been doing to address these issues haven't worked terribly well.

All in all, I've come away from my visit encouraged. It feels comforting to put myself in the hands of folks who have expertise I lack. One of the mistakes I made in preparing for my first Ironman was trying to do it all on my own. With the arrogance of youth, I believed I could achieve my goals by virtue of talent, hard work, and my own expertise. And while these things did take me fairly far, I could have gone further with a little help.

To surpass my younger self, I need to exploit the advantages of age in ways that compensate for the disadvantages, and for me this is largely a matter of acceptance. For the most part, I don't feel old, but at times I do, like when I attempt full-tilt, out-of-the-saddle hill sprints on my road bike. I just don't have the power I once had, and I accept that no amount of hard work will entirely restore it. But I'm not resigned to slowing down on the racecourse just because I've lost a little zip. One thing I have at 47 that I lacked at 31 is humility. I've learned to accept the limitations of my knowledge and get help when I need it, and I intend to ask for plenty more before this journey is complete.

4

EMBRACING REALITY

Freedom is what we do with what is done to us.
JEAN-PAUL SARTRE

IN THE BEGINNING, Rob Krar didn't know he was depressed—he thought he was just unhappy. And he *was* unhappy, with plenty of reason to be. Raised in the forested port city of Hamilton, Ontario, where he enjoyed an outdoorsy lifestyle filled with cross-country ski excursions and canoeing trips, he relocated to treeless, landlocked Phoenix in 2002 to take a job working graveyard shifts as a pharmacist, which he hated. A gifted endurance athlete who twice qualified for the Canadian Junior National Triathlon Team and later ran on scholarship at Butler University in Indianapolis, he'd quit the sport upon completing his studies, burned out on the old motivations of (as he described them to me) "keeping up with the neighbors, impressing others," not realizing there were other reasons to get out and sweat, and missing it more than he knew. A life-of-the-party kind of guy in high school, he struggled to make friends in his new environment. In fact, he had only one—two if you counted his girlfriend, but their relationship was unraveling.

It wasn't until Rob moved to Flagstaff in 2006—a change of scenery he undertook for the sole purpose of studying for Canada's pharmacy board exam so he could then flee home to Hamilton as soon as possible—that he realized, by degrees, he had a mental illness. In Flagstaff, Rob rediscovered his love of the outdoors, made lots of friends, and got back into running. But he still wasn't happy. Yet he wasn't merely unhappy, either. He was depressed.

Running is proven to help with depression, but it didn't help Rob, and wouldn't until he got past those old, externally focused motivations. In 2007, he finished 27th in the Boston Marathon, overcoming sleet and 20 mph headwinds to record a superb debut time of 2:25:44, but in his relentless quest to keep up with the neighbors and impress others, Rob resumed heavy training before his body was ready and spent the better part of the next three years battling injuries.

In 2010, beset by chronic pain in both heels that bothered him even when he was standing behind the pharmacy desk at Walgreens, Rob was persuaded by his friend Mike Smith (an Olympic Trials Marathon qualifier who now serves as the head cross country and track coach at Northern Arizona University) to try his hand at trail racing, specifically the TransRockies Run, a six-day race for two-person teams. Unable to run a single step in the five days preceding the event—indeed, unable to even warm up before the first stage—Rob somehow got through day one. In first place. The second day, still leading the competition with Mike, he leveraged the attention his gutty performance was garnering to chat up Christina Bauer, a runner in the women's team division who'd caught his eye. As Rob made his approach, it struck him that he had no idea what he was going to say, so he offered her one of the free lip balms the race organizer was handing out.

"How about these ChapSticks?" he said, showing his winningest smile.

An awkward silence followed as Christina studied the gift in the way a forensic art investigator might inspect an obvious forgery.

"I do *not* put petroleum-based products on my lips," she said eventually, handing the tube back.

Ouch! But it all worked out. Rob and Mike won the race, Rob and Christina started dating, and Rob quit running a second time, a decision that was all but forced on him by the failure of double surgery to alleviate his heel pain, yet one that offered the consolation of allowing him to focus on his relationship with Christina. They went on hiking and camping trips together, learned to fly fish, did a lot of ski mountaineering in the winter, and talked about absolutely everything—including his depression.

Christina, meanwhile, continued to run, and in February 2012, four months before she and Rob tied the knot, she talked him into tagging along for a 33-kilometer trail race despite his not having run in two years. Remarkably, he was able to complete the entire distance. In first place.

At this point, the old Rob would have been unable to resist getting sucked back into running with his prior motivations. The new Rob saw the restoration of his ability to run as a gift, a precious and fragile blessing that he wished to honor by racing not for respect or attention as before but for the inner journey, and by listening to his body and respecting rest, and also by investing himself in the trail running community.

In November of that same year, Rob did his first official ultramarathon, the Bootlegger 50K in Boulder City, Nevada. Late in the race he began to struggle, and his inner journey took him somewhere he'd never been before: the "dark place," as he now calls it, a place of intense suffering and deep ambivalence—that desperate tug-of-war between the desire to persevere and the overwhelming temptation to quit. And he loved it. A living hell to most, this dark place felt to Rob like home, uncanny in its similarity to his experience of depression, but with one key difference: control.

"When I get late into a race," Rob explained in a 2018 interview with podcaster Billy Yang, "and it hurts the most and I'm questioning how I'm going to make it to the finish line, there's a certain darkness that I can relate to when I struggle to get out the door for a run, or when it's at its very worst, when I feel helpless and worthless. Now I'm in a position where I feel kind of similar, but I'm in control. I can make the pain stop at any moment. I can stop. I can walk. I can quit. But I choose to keep going, and it's this incredible, cathartic experience that I very rarely have the opportunity to have."

Lots of runners get hooked on ultras from their first taste. For Rob it was that times 20, a "Where have you been all my life?" sort of thing. In April 2013, he ran the Leona Divide 50 Mile, winning by an almost comical margin and shattering the course record. A month later, he eclipsed the fastest known time for the "rim to rim to rim" crossing of the Grand Canyon, covering 42 unforgiving miles in 6 hours and 21 minutes, destroying the old mark. A few weeks later, in June, he claimed second place in the Western States 100, the Super Bowl of 100 milers and his debut, unveiling what would become his signature racing style—patient and pursuant—hounding down a flagging Timothy Olson in the waning miles of the race to finish less than five minutes behind him.

In the next two years, Rob returned to Western States and won, and then won the almost equally hallowed Leadville Trail 100, won Western States again, was named 2014 and 2015 Ultra Runner of the Year, started a running camp business, and gave up his pharmacy job to become a sponsored full-time professional athlete at age 38. But these dreamlike highs were counterbalanced by nightmarish plunges into "the hole," as Rob refers to his depressive episodes, emotional freefalls often triggered by injuries, to which he remained frustratingly susceptible despite his wiser approach to the sport.

In November 2017, Rob found himself in his deepest hole yet, the darkest of dark places, with seemingly no way out. It began with a single false step in the final mile of the North Face Endurance Challenge 50K in Ontario, his beloved old stomping grounds. Rob's right knee briefly hyperextended on impact and essentially exploded, a marble-size chunk of cartilage obliterated like so much fissile material. He somehow managed to complete the race (in first place), but two weeks later he was on an operating table in Flagstaff, and two days after that, he was a veritable bubble boy, spending eight hours a day prostrate on his living room floor with his leg trapped in a continuous passive motion (CPM) machine, watching Netflix while his cats made a nest of his inert body. He rose only to use the bathroom, fetch food from the kitchen, and, if necessary, take out the garbage or collect the day's mail—all with the help of crutches (later a cane).

That's no life for anyone, much less a runner. Much less a runner susceptible to depression. After 20 days, Rob was released from his CPM imprisonment, but by then a neurochemical switch had been flipped, and his emancipation lifted him only two feet, literally—from the floor to the couch, a rust-colored leather upholstered relic from the lost years in Phoenix—where he continued to lay prostrate for eight hours on most days, as though still trapped in the machine. What was the point in getting up? He couldn't see one. In his heart of hearts, Rob knew he would never be happy again, let alone run again.

Buck Blankenship, Rob's friend and training partner, was able to gauge how Rob was doing based on his response time to text messages. As summer faded into fall, the lag extended from minutes to hours to days. Ryan Whited, Rob's strength coach and the only human other than Christina who saw Rob frequently during this period, could tell how Rob was doing just by the look in his eyes when he limped through the door of Paragon Athletics in east Flagstaff. As time went on, the look in Rob's eyes changed from penetrating (normal) to empty (red flag).

Such circumstances will strain any marriage, and Rob and Christina's was no exception. Not wanting to take his wife down with him, Rob told her she'd be better off without him, a message she couldn't help but interpret as his way of saying *he'd* be better off without *her*. Further complicating matters was the fact that, by right and by necessity, Christina had her own life to live—a demanding job as an academic and career advisor, intensive training for the Run Rabbit Run 100-Mile Race, family members dealing with crises of their own and needing her support—and couldn't be there for her husband 24-7 even if he wanted her to be.

It was with no small degree of trepidation that Christina left Rob alone at home on the second weekend of November and flew east for an overdue visit to celebrate her father's birthday. Rob spent all of that Saturday lying on the couch doing just what Christina feared he might be doing in her absence: thinking about ending his life. Never much of a drinker, he'd become more of one lately, and he threw back a few G&Ts that evening, not so much to escape his melancholy as to wallow in it.

Rob had reached a point where, perversely, he wanted to feel more, not less, of the darkness inside him. In service to this agenda, he cued up the last episode of the Netflix series *Hell on Wheels* on his laptop, a melancholy hour that ended with a tragic murder. He'd watched it many times already. It featured the Duhks's cover of the Kat Goldman song "Annabel," a darkly gorgeous folk lament with lyrics like these: "Tell me where does the spirit go when you die? / Oh where does the spirit go when you die?"

When the show ended, Rob pointed his web browser to Google and typed in a series of keyword searches:

> *best gun for suicide*
> *buying gun with green card*
> *are gun stores open on sundays*

Scrolling past the urgent help offers from the National Suicide Prevention Lifeline that always come up first when such searches are performed, Rob was able to ascertain that pretty much any firearm a person might use to end his life has both advantages and disadvantages, that he could legally purchase a gun in Arizona as a green-card-holding Canadian citizen, and that he could do so as soon as the next day if he so wished. In fact, though, Rob had no intention of buying a pistol (or a shotgun) and killing himself the next day. Just knowing he had the option gave him a measure of comfort, a fallback in case he couldn't hang on until his next running camp, then eight weeks away, which he looked to as a possible escape route from the hole.

Rob described these events to me in unflinching detail, speaking with almost clinical neutrality, eschewing both self-pity and bravado, when I visited Flagstaff to take part in one of his camps—not the one that indeed became the turning point in his physical and emotional recovery but one that took place several months later. As I listened to him, I was reminded of a moment in Rob's 2014 documentary video "Depressions: A Few Moments from 30 Miles in the Canyon." A handheld camera shows Rob from behind as he charges up the Grand Canyon's south wall, awestruck tourists leaping out of his path, his disembodied voice narrating: "The biggest change for me is to accept that I'm going in the hole and embrace it. I allow myself to think about it. *Yeah, this really sucks, and I wish this didn't happen to me.* That's been a huge change and coping strategy to me. I've been able to shorten the episodes to as short as a day sometimes."

Being caught in a deep depression is a little like being strapped down by your wrists and ankles and tortured by a strong, pitiless villain. You have almost no control over the situation. The one thing you can do to gain some measure of victory over your tormentor is to embrace what's happening—to welcome it, perhaps even convince the villain that you're enjoying it, just to spite him: watch a gloomy television show; listen to a sad song; go through the exercise of researching suicide methods, even if you have no immediate intention of acting on what you learn. Such last-ditch measures to resist what's happening might make the situation only 1 percent more bearable, but heck, Tim Olson's margin of victory over Rob Krar in the 2013 Western States 100 was less than half of 1 percent.

In life and in sport, there are times when a small difference makes all the difference. Rob's visits to the dark place during races have enabled him to cope just a little better with depression by helping him embrace the hole. Indeed, psychologists have a name for this coping technique: trauma mastery. In their book, *Trauma Stewardship*, Laura van Dernoot Lipsky and Connie Burk write, "For many survivors of trauma, our lack of control over a traumatic incident is one of the most terrifying and unnerving things about it . . . What humans often do to reconcile this lack of control is to create and re-create situations as similar to the traumatic incident as possible. We seek to turn a traumatic situation in which we once felt powerless into a new situation where we feel competent and in charge."

In Rob's case, not only does ultrarunning help him master the trauma of depressive episodes, but his efforts to master these episodes in turn help him master the mental challenges of ultrarunning. "I've been able to go to a place in these ultras that I've never been able to before," Rob says in the "Depressions" video. "The way I'm better able to cope with these episodes is I embrace it. I allow it to happen. People say, 'You've just got to fight the pain, you've got to ignore the pain.' And I'm just the opposite. When I get to that point late in a race where I'm struggling and my body's shutting down and my mind just wants to stop, I embrace it."

THREE STEPS TO EMBRACING REALITY

The idea of embracing a bad situation may sound masochistic, but it's not. To embrace a depressive episode or hitting the wall in a race is not to take pleasure in it, but rather (to use Rob Krar's word) to cope with it. Having accepted the reality of a bad situation, an athlete has the option to either give in to it or try to make the best of it. Embracing the reality of a bad situation entails committing to making the best of it. There are times, of course, when the best that can be made of a bad situation doesn't look a whole lot different from the bad situation itself—Rob's 2017 depressive episode being a prime example. But, again, sometimes a small difference makes all the difference.

Some athletes are really good at embracing reality; others are not so good. Studies involving deceptive performance feedback offer one way of measuring an athlete's capacity to embrace reality. In one such study, led by Mark Stone of Buckinghamshire New University and published in *PLoS One* in 2017, 10 male cyclists were asked to complete a series of simulated 4,000-meter time trials on stationary bikes. The first time trial was used to establish a performance baseline. In two others, the cyclists competed against an avatar that they were told represented their baseline performance, but in fact the avatar performed 2 percent better in one of these deceptive tests and 5 percent better in the other.

When competing against a 2 percent superior version of themselves, all 10 cyclists succeeded in completing the distance more quickly than before. But when matched against the 5 percent superior version, only a couple of cyclists achieved their best result (although none actually kept up with the avatar), while a few others performed about the same as, or slightly worse than, they had in the other, less extreme deceptive test, and the rest performed even worse than they had in the baseline test, two of them significantly so.

To me, the most interesting subjects in this experiment are the pair who performed worse in the 5 percent test than in the 2 percent test but still better than in the baseline test. These cyclists must have realized early on that they were going to fail—that, for reasons unknown to them, they just didn't have the legs to keep up with the avatar that supposedly represented their own baseline performance. And yet they didn't give up. Instead, they accepted the inevitability of falling short and then embraced the situation by doing the best they could, which, also unbeknownst to them, was in fact better than their baseline performance. Whatever it is that it takes to commit to making the best of an athletic experience that is doomed to not turn out as hoped, these guys had it.

So, what does it take? Three specific psychological mindsets show up again and again in athletes who habitually choose to try to make lemonade from the lemons they are dealt in training, competition, and life:

1) Internal locus of control
2) Growth mindset
3) Positivity/gratitude

The good news for athletes who aren't so good at embracing a bad situation is that all of these mindsets can be nurtured over time. The first step is understanding them—a step we'll take together now.

Internal Locus of Control

It goes without saying that in order to commit to making the best of a bad situation, you have to believe you have the power to change it. Not everyone believes they have this power. The term *locus of control* refers to where individuals place responsibility for their successes and failures. Individuals who have an internal locus of control see themselves as having the capacity to achieve their goals by their own initiative in most situations, even if external forces are working against them. Individuals with an external locus of control see themselves as being dependent on favorable external forces to succeed in challenging situations.

Research has shown that "internals" and "externals" have different ways of coping with stressful events and that coping methods favored by internals typically yield better results. Among the pioneers in this area of research was Carl Anderson of the University of Maryland. His best-known study, published in the *Journal of Applied Psychology* in 1977, involved 90 business owners whose coping methods Anderson observed for a period of two and a half years following a "major disaster" affecting their business. At the beginning of this period, all 90 owners completed tests designed to assess their locus of control. After analyzing the data he collected, Anderson reported that "Internals were found to perceive less stress, employ more task-centered coping behaviors, and employ fewer emotion-centered coping behaviors than externals." Task-centered coping behaviors are simply practical actions taken to solve or limit the impact of the source of present stress (e.g., fetching a fire extinguisher in response to fire), whereas emotion-centered coping behaviors include avoidance, apathy, and anxiety (e.g., screaming, "Fire! Somebody do something!").

Let's look at an example of how an internal locus of control and its associated coping skills can help someone embrace, and thereby make the best of, a bad situation in the endurance sports context. On July 11, 1999, professional triathlete Stefan Laursen was on his way home to Delray Beach, Florida, from a training stint at Lake Tahoe when stormy weather turned what was supposed to have been a short layover at Houston International Airport into a six-hour encampment. Worse, upon finally arriving in Florida late that night, Stefan discovered that the airline had lost both his bike and his gear bag. A nuisance under any circumstances, the screwup was especially problematic in Stefan's immediate circumstances, as he was supposed to compete in the Coca-Cola Classic Triathlon in Boca Raton the next morning. At this point, an athlete with an external locus of control might have thought, *There's no way I can do tomorrow's race without my bike.* But Stefan believed it wasn't his bike but his legs that made him competitive, so he borrowed a bike and shoes from a friend, slept for two hours, and won the race.

In bad situations, externals get discouraged, and internals get resourceful, putting their energy into managing the problem itself rather than their emotions. This is what Rob Krar did in coming back from his knee surgery. His first few tentative strides were taken in February 2018 in the company of attendees of his winter running camp, but many more weeks would pass before he was able to return to full training. Understanding the necessity of being resourceful, Rob reminded himself that it wasn't running per se but being outdoors and pushing his body and mind that he really needed, so he dusted off his mountain bike and rode the heck out of it. In August, he raced the Leadville 100 Trail MTB, a 104-mile mountain bike race that takes place a week before the eponymous ultramarathon he'd won in 2014, finishing 14th in a field of 1,644, among the top athletes in a sport that wasn't even his sport.

There are five proven ways to cultivate an internal locus of control like Stefan Laursen's and Rob Krar's:

1) Focus on what you can control. Having an internal locus of control does not mean believing you're in control of everything. The problem for externals is that they believe they have less control than they do. To avoid this situation, consciously enumerate—even write down—the factors that you *can* control whenever something goes wrong or threatens to spoil your training or racing. For example, suppose you're training for an early-season triathlon and a friend comes home after a course reconnaissance trip three weeks before the event and reports that the lake water temperature is a bone-chilling 57 degrees. In this scenario, an external is likely to become anxious and spend a lot of time hoping the lake warms up in the next three weeks. But no one can control the weather. Your time and emotional energy are better spent considering sensible equipment changes (e.g., neoprene swim cap), finding ways to practice swimming in cold water, and mentally bracing for a cold swim.

2) Censor yourself. Certain self-limiting words and phrases appear repeatedly in the thoughts and speech of externals during stressful moments. These include "can't," "impossible," "I wish," and "What's the use?" Banish such expressions of helplessness from your thoughts and speech and replace them with alternatives that put you in the driver's seat. For example, replace "There's no way I can get down to my competition weight for January's race with the holidays coming up" with "With the holidays coming up, I need to make a concrete plan for getting down to my competition weight for January's race."

3) Pivot from problem to solution. Externals are prone to fixate on problems while internals tend to shift quickly from recognizing a problem to identifying solutions. In my coaching work, I never allow an athlete to spend more time than necessary describing or discussing the nature of a problem. When I see an athlete start to go down this path, I step in and ask, "So, what do we do about it?" You can do the same for yourself. It's okay and even necessary to consider a problem long enough to properly define it, but once that's done, it's time to start thinking about fixes.

4) Don't think in all-or-nothing terms. Before she died of cancer at 32 years of age, American middle-distance runner Gabriele Grunewald told an interviewer, "It's worth doing even if it's not perfect. And I think sometimes we're too quick to give up on the things that we love and the things that make us feel alive when something is going wrong in our lives, but I just feel really strongly that we have to hold on to them." One of the reasons externals give up on their dreams too quickly is that when an obstacle comes along and renders a dream unrealizable, they are not able to imagine any other outcome that makes the best of the situation. It's all or nothing.

Gabe didn't have this mindset. She finished in last place in her final race (an opening-round 1500-meter heat at the US championships) in 2017—a race she ran during a two-week break between chemotherapy treatments. Having won a national title at 3,000 meters three years before, Gabe would surely have much preferred to win again on this occasion, then go on to win the semifinal and the final, and then go on to earn a medal in the same event at the world championships in London. Cancer, however, placed such ambitions out of reach. Yet if Gabe hadn't committed to making the best of the situation, she wouldn't have even made it to the start line of that last race, which became something more than a race when the crowd gave her a standing ovation as she finished alone and her fellow competitors then huddled around her to pray and shower her with love. The next time a setback tempts you to revert from the "all" of your next big goal to the "nothing" of giving up, remember Gabe Grunewald.

5) Ask for help. There's no law that says you have to go it alone when facing challenges. Getting help from others is not the same thing as leaving yourself dependent on outside forces. Rather, it is one of the task-centered coping methods that internals use to solve problems, as Stefan Laursen did in borrowing a bike and shoes from a friend so he could race the Coca-Cola Classic. No matter how good your coping skills are, you can't solve some problems without a little help. Don't hold back from getting the help you need when you find yourself in a bad situation you can't get out of alone.

Growth Mindset

The second mindset that strongly affects our ability to embrace bad situations has to do with how challenges are perceived. Psychologist Carol Dweck and her colleagues at Stanford University have demonstrated that whether a person believes intelligence and other abilities are fixed or can be increased through hard work has profound implications for their success in school and elsewhere. Those who tend to see their abilities as unchanging have what Dweck calls a "fixed mindset," and they struggle to embrace challenges. Those who believe that through hard work they can increase not just their knowledge or skill in some area but their underlying ability have a "growth mindset," and they readily embrace challenges.

You might assume that all athletes have a growth mindset. After all, sports are challenging by their very nature, and the time and effort athletes put into training are predicated on the belief that through hard work they can increase their fitness and performance. But although athletes as a group may be more growth-minded than the general population, some are more growth-minded than others.

In my coaching work, I see this most plainly in the different ways athletes approach challenging workouts. According to Dweck, the reason folks with a fixed mindset don't like challenges is that they view them as tests, the results of which pass permanent judgment on their ability. Over the years, I have worked with a number of athletes who clearly viewed their harder workouts as tests. These athletes typically experience intense anxiety before and throughout these workouts, an unpleasant emotional state that harms performance. They are also more likely than other athletes to push harder than they should to hit their numbers on days when circumstances are against them or their body just doesn't have it. Additionally, these athletes are quick to hit the panic button when a tough session doesn't turn out well, suffering a crisis of confidence that often precipitates bad decisions.

I once received an email message with the subject line "Pounding the Panic Button with a Sledgehammer" from an athlete who was following a custom training plan I'd built for him. On reading the body of the message, I learned that the athlete had just bombed a long, marathon-pace workout after many weeks of problem-free training. One bad workout in an otherwise smooth training cycle and the poor fellow was "pounding the panic button with a sledgehammer"? That's the fixed mindset for you.

Athletes who have a growth mindset view challenging workouts not as tests but as stimuli, whose purpose is to provide an earned benefit, not to pass judgment. If they crank out numbers that attract lots of kudos from their Strava followers, so much the better, but they know the workout served its purpose regardless. In my experience, athletes who have this perspective don't get as anxious before important sessions, they don't force things unwisely when circumstances are unfavorable or their body just doesn't have it that day, and they're less prone to panic when a session goes poorly.

When working with athletes who have a fixed mindset, I offer up little mantras they can use to shift from an outcome orientation to a process orientation during challenging workouts. Here are a few of my favorites:

"Just do the work." This is a blunt self-reminder that a workout's true purpose is in the doing, and that the benefits result from simply getting it done, irrespective of how you feel or perform.

"It doesn't all have to happen today." Too often, athletes get anxious when their performance in a challenging workout reveals how far they have to go to achieve a goal. Such anxiety is based on a fixed-mindset tendency to forget that, unless your next big race is tomorrow, it's not how fit you are today that matters but whether you're getting fitter, and challenging workouts make you fitter, regardless of what they may say about your current fitness.

"Check the box and move on." Not every workout can be a transcendent breakthrough experience. But even the ones you have to grind through have value—indeed, no less value than the transcendent breakthroughs do as stepping-stones toward your ultimate goal. I've found this mantra works well to dispel the frustration that might otherwise attach itself to workouts that are a struggle.

It's worth noting that hard workouts are *chosen* challenges. Athletes plan and execute them willingly. Many challenges we face as athletes—and indeed as humans—are not chosen, and here the growth mindset makes an even bigger difference. As we've seen, many athletes recoil from unexpected setbacks in a variety of ways, but growth-minded athletes tend to embrace these events, too, as opportunities to move forward.

In the 1990s, UNC psychologists Richard Tedeschi and Lawrence Calhoun coined the term *post-traumatic growth* (PTG) to label "the experience of positive change resulting from the struggle with major life crises." Since then, a number of studies have found that a substantial fraction of individuals who endure a major life crisis later see themselves as having been changed for the better by it, citing benefits that include new opportunities or possibilities in life, an increased sense of personal strength, positive changes in their relationships with others, a greater appreciation for life in general, and an enriched spiritual life.

Not everyone grows through suffering, however. When asked in a 2012 interview for brainline.com who *does* experience post-traumatic growth, Tedeschi said, "I'd say the type of people who may tend to experience PTG are those who would actively approach difficulty rather an avoid it. Someone who is open to change, open to the novelty and serendipity of life. People who can accept that bad things happen, that they can no longer do certain things, but who focus on engaging in the things that they can still do. And people who are open to new opportunities . . . possibilities and choices that may not have presented themselves before the tragedy." Sounds a lot like Dweck's growth mindset, doesn't it?

To be clear, it's not the traumatic experience itself but how some people process it that yields growth. The growth-minded way to process unchosen challenges is to *narrativize* them, investing them with a particular meaning that furthers your progress toward a happy ending to your personal story, even if it's not the ending you planned originally. Rob Krar considers himself more open, more present, and more resilient today than he was before his injuries and depressive episodes, and now that he's got these enhanced qualities, he wouldn't want to give them up. "It's not like I wish these things upon myself," he told me, but neither does he wish they hadn't happened, because they've become meaningful parts of his unique story.

No trauma is too great to narrativize in a way that makes something better of it. In an interview she did with *The Morning Shakeout* podcast host Mario Fraioli several months before her death, Gabe Grunewald said this: "I do think that my life has a purpose—and maybe it's not what I thought it was going to be, but I think that it does help me at some junctures with this disease. This isn't how I would have chosen my life to turn out at all, but maybe this is my way of fulfilling my life's purpose and trying to raise awareness for these rare diseases that really do actually need it. I would never have raised my hand to do this, but someone has to." Talk about turning lemons into lemonade.

You need not have depression or cancer to benefit from narrativizing your struggles and cultivating a growth mindset. Thinking of your athletic journey—which is inseparable from your overall life journey—as a story, and interpreting the challenges you experience as necessary steps in this journey, will help you embrace all manner of bad situations and make the best of them.

Positivity/Gratitude

A third way in which ultrarealists embrace bad situations is by seeing them as not *all* bad. In even the worst moments, a lot is happening. Each slice of conscious experience has layers and facets, and they're truly never all bad simultaneously. Those with a positive mindset tend to focus on the silver lining of an overall bad situation, which helps them embrace it.

Psychologists refer to this skill as cognitive restructuring or cognitive reframing, the first term applying to the technique's formal use in therapy and the second to its informal use in everyday life. I like to think of cognitive reframing as finding the most helpful interpretation of a bad situation—a way of seeing it that preserves hope for an acceptable outcome. This makes it quite different from mere spin, like the Black Knight saying to King Arthur in *Monty Python and the Holy Grail* after his entire arm is hacked off, "'Tis but a scratch." To be truly helpful, a positive reframing of a bad situation cannot be untruthful. You're changing the *frame*, not the picture.

When Rob Krar was laid up with his knee injury, he told himself, "I've never had an injury that I didn't come back from stronger and wiser than before." He didn't lie to himself by pretending he wasn't injured or that coming back would be easy. Rather, he steered his thoughts away from the pain and frustration of the injury and toward the most helpful, hopeful true thing about the situation he could conjure.

Another mantra that I encourage athletes to use in hard moments is "I've been here before." Repeat this phrase when you find yourself struggling in a way you've struggled in the past and gotten through. For example, if you hit a bad patch in a race, remind yourself that you have experienced similar moments in even your best races.

To take the positive mindset a step further, practice gratitude. Whereas general positivity entails finding the good within a bad situation, gratitude entails putting a bad situation in a broader context, specifically a context that reminds you how much worse things could be. It's no accident that some of the greatest masters of gratitude are survivors of near-death experiences, who are able to say in almost any bad situation, "At least I'm alive!" Research by psychologist Araceli Frias of Eastern Washington University and others suggests that, as with post-traumatic growth, it's not the scare itself but the subsequent perspective shift that enhances gratitude. In a 2011 paper published in *The Journal of Positive Psychology*, for example, Frias reported that subjects who were asked to spend structured time reflecting on death experienced an increase in gratitude.

The athletic equivalent of a brush with death is an injury or illness that takes away one's ability to do the sport one loves, and it often has the same effect. In August 2018, American professional runner Sarah Crouch underwent an operation to remove a tumor in her left quadriceps. Though technically benign, the growth was so large and deep that her surgeon couldn't promise the then 29-year-old that she would be able to return to running afterward. On the advice of a friend, Sarah went for a run in her favorite Flagstaff training venue the day before the operation. Running had never seemed so precious to her as it did in that solitary hour.

Less than two months later, still sporting stitches and a bandage where she'd been cut open, Sarah stood on the start line of the Chicago Marathon, happy just to be there—a marked change from the year before, when she stood on the same start line thinking, *Why do I do this to myself?* Cold and wet conditions wrought havoc on much of the elite field in 2018, but Sarah's grateful mindset enabled her to not only survive the battle of attrition but finish sixth overall and first among Americans with a seven-second personal best.

"It had never really occurred to me that running was a choice," she told me later. "Only when the option to make that choice was threatened in that hospital room did I truly appreciate how much I actually did want to be out there running a marathon and hurting like hell."

As Araceli Frias's study indicates, it is not necessary to have a brush with death—or to be threatened with the permanent loss of your ability to do the sport you love—to become more grateful. All you have to do is make a regular practice of cataloging things you're grateful for or writing letters of gratitude. I like to give thanks in an informal way during workouts and races, and I encourage my athletes to do the same. If you're cruising along the trail and feeling good on a beautiful fall day, don't take these things for granted—give thanks for them. If you complete a familiar hill climb on your bike and feel a pinch of disappointment when you see a substandard time for the ascent, remind yourself that you're healthy and training and getting fitter. These thoughts won't merely make the training and racing experience more enjoyable; in the long run, they will also make you faster.

True black belts of gratitude like Rob Krar are able to embrace parts of the sporting experience that few others do. In 2015, Rob suffered a low-back injury that led to the diagnosis and correction of a pelvic imbalance he otherwise wouldn't have known he had. Rob was consciously grateful for the injury, knowing it would make him a more durable athlete in the future.

After I signed up for Rob's fall 2018 running camp, I began to receive e-newsletters that he sent out to all of the registrants. The opening sentence of the first of these read as follows: "This idea of hosting a running camp originated from a feeling of gratitude—as my ultrarunning career took off by surprise, I recognized how important my home and my community had been, and continue to be, to my success and how significant their roles have been in my journey."

This sentiment was corroborated by the camp experience itself. I've been to a lot of running camps, and they all have swag, but Rob's was like Christmas. I'm still using some of the stuff I got there. But it wasn't just swag for swag's sake—every item was thoughtfully chosen to meet a need that would come up during the camp, from the anti-chafing stick to the various solutions for post-run carb cravings. We were equally spoiled by the meals, many of which were homecooked by Christina and worthy of photographing before you dug in.

I studied Rob closely throughout that weekend. He was so engaged, so "on," that it was difficult to imagine him in a hole, and I guess that's the idea. For him, the camps provide a mission that makes his running bigger than himself, and a reason to keep going. The camp that came eight weeks after his darkest hour may well have rescued Rob, but if it did, he wasn't alone. More than one camper dealing with depression and suicidal thoughts has told Rob the experience saved their own life.

Rob's journey from his first postsurgical run—a run he saved especially for the camp that became his turning point—to the start line of the 2018 Leadville Trail 100, which took place only seven days after he pedaled his way to 14th place in the Leadville Trail 100 MTB, was a journey of gratitude. His decision to participate was spontaneous, made earlier in the same week, when he discovered that his legs felt surprisingly okay during a six-mile jog. He had never started a 100-mile race less prepared physically, but he didn't care. He was happy just to be there.

The race began in a predawn darkness defied by 712 headlamps. Rob started with his usual patience, feeling as if he were floating as he strode along the Boulevard, a feeling that, as it turned out, did not abate. At 24 miles, exiting the Outward Bound aid station, he slipped into the lead, schooling the less patient. From there, Rob proceeded to set an all-time record for the punishing 3,400-foot ascent from Twin Lakes to Hope Pass—running those five miles faster than anyone else ever had, even on fresh legs—and by the time he hit the pass again, inbound, he was near course-record pace. *How lucky am I to be out here?* he thought at 12,508 feet.

Cruising through Twin Lakes again, Rob saw thousands of jubilant faces, and heard a roar he'd only ever heard before in sports arenas back in Ontario, seemingly far more fans making far more racket than when he won five years earlier. But it wasn't the size of the crowd that had changed; it was Rob. That's how gratitude works, transforming not reality itself but how reality is seen.

He crossed the finish line nearly *two hours* ahead of the runner-up. Photos taken at the moment he raised the winner's banner overhead show him with his eyes closed, face lifted to the sky, lips parted in a grimace-smile that is a mix of exhausted relief, triumph, and thanks. If embracing reality, in all its imperfection, has a face, Rob Krar was wearing it.

5½ MONTHS TO SANTA ROSA

I had my swim first lesson today—my first, that is, with my new instructor, Mandy. We met at 6:30 a.m. in San Bruno, a small city located on the southern base of the San Francisco Peninsula, more than 100 miles from my home in the Central Valley. So you can imagine how early I had to get out of bed, and if you can't, I'll tell you: 3:50.

I discovered Mandy through an online search that was instigated by my frustration at how little progress I've made in the five months since I started swimming. My goal is to complete the swim leg of Ironman Santa Rosa in less than 60 minutes, and it has become apparent that I will not achieve this goal without expert help. It would be nice if getting the help I need didn't require predawn wakeups, but as I struggled through rush-hour traffic this morning, emails piling up in my inbox and an untouched to-do list waiting on my day planner back home, I tried to embrace the hassle as a symbol of my dedication to this endeavor.

One thing that gives me confidence that the hassle will prove worthwhile is that I've done this before. When I started racing triathlons in the late 1990s, I made the classic runner-turned-triathlete mistake of assuming I could become a good swimmer the same way I'd become a good runner: by getting fit. But swimming isn't as much about fitness as about technique, and after four years of grinding out laps on my own, I was only marginally more adept in the water than I'd been on day one, so I hired a coach to video-tape my stroke and give me some pointers that I then took home and prac-ticed. I'll never forget the moment it all came together. After half a decade of treading water, so to speak, I went from being a mediocre swimmer to a pretty good one (by triathlon standards, anyway) literally in the time it takes to snap your fingers, and in my next race I posted the seventh-fastest swim in my age group.

Alas, I put triathlon on hold soon thereafter to focus on marathon training, and when I got back in the pool in 2004, I discovered I'd reverted to my prior, mediocre form, and I've been unable to find the old magic ever since. I explained all of this to Mandy on the deck of a tiny indoor pool located inside the community center of the apartment complex where she lives and

gives lessons. She absorbed the information with minimal comment, perhaps reserving the right to make her own judgment about how to make me a
better swimmer.

We started off with a few dryland drills intended to improve my body position and posture: standing tall with my chin slightly tucked and my belly button drawn inward; raising my arms overhead while focusing on keeping my
arms and head in three separate "lanes"; dropping the left arm while rotating
the hips to the right, then doing the reverse. Mandy told me to do these exercises regularly in front of the bathroom mirror at home, and I will.

In the water, Mandy took me through moving versions of the dryland drills
she'd just shown me and then had me swim a few laps while she scrutinized
my technique. Pronouncing my stroke "pretty good overall," she proceeded to
enumerate several ways to improve it. These include relaxing my shoulders,
which will allow my arms to move more freely and engage my stronger back
muscles in the pull phase; pointing my toes slightly inward when I kick; and
flinging the recovering arm away from my body with an extended elbow so that
it circles around by its own momentum and doesn't affect my posture. Lastly,
Mandy filmed me practicing these technique modifications.

Driving home from the lesson, I felt a vague dissatisfaction. Its source,
I soon realized, was Mandy's failure to address what I consider to be the defining flaw in my stroke, which is poor body position. Sixteen years ago, when I
went from being a mediocre swimmer to a pretty good one in the time it takes
to snap your fingers, I did it by discovering a way to get my hips to sit higher in
the water so that my lower body created less drag. The effect was palpable
and measurable; in a single instant, swimming became effortless, and I
counted two fewer strokes in crossing from one end of the pool to the other. It's
not that I thought Mandy's advice is bad—heck, she's forgotten more about
swimming than I will ever know—but it seemed to me to fall short of getting to
the heart of the problem.

Or did it? After several minutes of brooding, my inner ombudsman stepped
in with a warning against attaching myself to the notion that only by recreating
that aha moment from 2003 can I again elevate my swimming back to pretty
good. When I last trained for triathlons in 2009, I drove myself nuts with my
fixation on doing just this—trying repeatedly to dredge up somatic memories

of how it all came together and recreate that moment. Time and again I went to the pool in a state of anxious hopefulness, having remembered something previously forgotten—something about pressing my face into the water, or gliding longer between strokes, or whatever—only to discover that it didn't work and return home disappointed.

An ultrarealist in my position wouldn't allow himself to fall into this trap, and I mustn't either. Ultrarealists don't waste time wishing for a different reality. Wishing I could get back to effortless swimming the same way I got there before was essentially wishing to go back in time. Whatever it was I did to improve my body position in 2003, it was a lucky guess, and only a fool allows his success to depend on luck, which is nonreplicable. The thing that made this bit of luck almost inevitable was a certain process, which *is* replicable, and which I am now replicating through my work with Mandy. I need to stay focused on this process and let it lead where it leads. It is entirely possible that I will arrive back at effortless swimming by a different route than I did before.

And something else: My prior efforts to rediscover the old magic drained all the fun out of swimming. In every stroke of every swim, I compared myself unfavorably to the swimmer I once was—a surefire recipe for nonenjoyment. I accept that enjoyment and aptitude are inextricably linked, and that I can't expect to enjoy swimming poorly as much as I once enjoyed swimming well, but it's important that I try to enjoy swimming as much as I can now, because I will spend hundreds of hours swimming between now and Ironman Santa Rosa, which is a lot of time to be miserable, and also because I believe the enjoyment-aptitude connection goes both ways, and if I prioritize enjoyment, aptitude will follow to some degree.

5

ADDRESSING REALITY

The impediment to action advances action.
What stands in the way becomes the way.
MARCUS AURELIUS

IN THE SUMMER OF 2007, I served on a four-man support crew for Dean Karnazes at the Badwater Ultramarathon, a 135-mile footrace from the sun-baked floor of Death Valley to the windswept upper slopes of Mount Whitney. On the eve of the competition, Dean and I attended a prerace meeting at a local elementary school. On the way in, Dean spotted someone he knew, a strikingly handsome man with a bald pate and a strapping physique.

"Do you know David Goggins?" Dean asked, nodding in the big fellow's direction. "No? You've got to meet this guy."

So we met, David showing zero interest in me and only slightly more interest in Dean—or perhaps laconic aloofness was just his style.

"Are you ready for tomorrow?" Dean asked him.

"Ready to get it over with," David said.

"He claims he hates running," Dean stage-whispered to me.

"I *do* hate running," David said.

And with that the two runners wished each other good luck and took seats on opposite sides of the auditorium.

The winner at Badwater three years earlier, Dean had a tough outing this time around, run-walking his way to a 10th-place finish. Linebacker-size David Goggins, meanwhile, took third.

Intrigued by this runner who hated running and yet willingly ran really far and exceedingly well, I looked him up later on YouTube, where I found a short interview recorded just after his podium finish. The camera shows him stone-faced, saying not a word, not even "Thanks," as Badwater race director Chris Kostman sits him down on a folding chair, drapes a medal around his neck, and congratulates him while a small crowd gathers around. Only when Kostman begins to ask direct questions does David begin to emerge from his aphasia.

"How do you feel?"

"I have nothing left," David mumbles, barely audible.

"Huge improvement in time over last year," Kostman prompts, hastening to fill an awkward silence. "Did you have a time goal coming into the race this year?"

"I just wanted to leave everything I had out there on that course," David says, showing a little more life, "and that's what I did."

My fascination with David Goggins only increased when, two years later, he was profiled in *Triathlete* magazine. In the article, David talked about how he went from disaffected youth to Navy SEAL to ultrarunner, delivering a number of bumper-sticker-worthy bon mots in the process, including this one, spoken in answer to a question about whether he took any supplements: "Yes, I take a giant suck-it-up pill every morning and wash it down with a refreshing can of hard."

David spent his early years in Buffalo, New York, and they were not happy years. The younger of two boys, he was subjected to horrific physical and psychological abuse by his father, who forced both boys and his wife to work six nights a week without pay at the roller-skating rink he owned, a nocturnal servitude that left young David unable to stay awake, think straight, or keep up in school. At home, he endured regular naked belt whippings, and when his father pulled a gun on him one afternoon, David realized he didn't care whether he lived or died. He was eight years old.

Not long after this incident, David's mother decided she'd had enough and fled to her parents' home in rural Indiana, taking her sons with her. Life didn't get much better for David in his new environment. Hopelessly far behind in school, he developed a debilitating stutter and lost half his hair—symptoms of what he would later learn was a condition called toxic stress syndrome. Racism compounded the problem. Conspicuously Black in an otherwise monochrome town, David found a death threat scrawled in his Spanish class notebook in the fall of his sophomore year of high school, and before the year was out, vandals had spray-painted the n-word on his car.

Seeing no viable way to succeed, David contributed to his own failure, skipping school frequently and getting cut from the varsity basketball team not for lack of ability but for lack of effort. College was not an option, so he enlisted in the Air Force with fantasies of becoming a pararescue specialist, but he couldn't handle the training program's water confidence test, and after four years he was a civilian again, a 297-pound recluse whose job was to kill pests at fast food restaurants—at night, naturally.

Who knows how long this purgatory might have lasted if David hadn't chanced upon a television documentary about the Navy SEALs one morning after a particularly soul-killing shift. The show focused on Hell Week, the famous 130-hour rite of passage that aspiring SEALs go through early in training to weed out wannabes. Watching the men of Class 224 suffer with such high purpose reignited David's warrior dreams, and the very next day he began calling recruiters. It took three weeks to find one who was willing to give him a chance, and it was a slim chance. David had six months to lose 106 pounds and pass an entrance exam.

Nothing short of a total commitment would make this challenge anything less than impossible, and David committed himself totally. He quit his job and with it his nocturnal lifestyle and adopted a regimen of nearly non-stop exercise, exhaustive study, and semi-starvation. On a typical day, he woke up at 4:30 a.m., rode a stationary bike for two hours while reading, swam for two hours, did a circuit strength workout, put in a couple more hours on the bike with a book in front of him, took a short break for a small dinner, and rode another two hours before going to bed. It was a punishing routine, but it worked. David made weight, passed the entrance exam, and joined BUD/S Class 230 on Coronado Island in January 2000.

One week into the 24-week program, David contracted double pneumonia. When instructors caught him hacking up bloody phlegm during a log-hauling drill, they pulled him off it, only to find him back under the log minutes later. After a third repetition of this sequence, David was yanked from training altogether and relegated to Class 231. On his second go, David somehow survived Hell Week with a wonky kneecap that, despite causing vomit-inducing pain, he was able to keep hidden until the docs ordered an X-ray that revealed a fracture and got him relegated to BUD/S Class 235— his last chance.

This time it was his feet: stress fractures, week three. They hurt even more than the broken patella, but David refused to let the pain stop him, and he survived to graduate at the top of his class on August 10, 2001— a month and a day before men like him would be needed more than ever.

There is some debate as to which is tougher: BUD/S or Army Ranger School. In 2004, after two deployments in Iraq with SEAL Team 5, David Goggins became one of the first men to complete both training programs. The following year, the deaths of five fellow SEALs in Afghanistan inspired David to do something in their honor, something extreme, and he settled on a 100-mile footrace in San Diego. At the time, he weighed 250 pounds (he'd gotten into powerlifting) and hadn't run farther than one mile in six months. But he knew how to suffer, and he completed the race with several broken metatarsals and kidney damage, having shat himself twice. David's remarkable feat of mind over matter not only raised a bunch of money for the Special Operations Warrior Foundation as intended but also qualified him for the 2006 Badwater Ultramarathon, where he placed fifth.

Seizing on the public attention David was gaining through running, the Navy hired him to help improve minority recruitment, which he did by traveling to schools and colleges and sharing his story. Meanwhile, he continued to compete in ultra-endurance races such as the Ultraman triathlon (a three-day event comprising a 6.2-mile swim, bike rides of 90 and 171.4 miles, and a 52.4-mile run) and Badwater.

The June 2009 issue of *Triathlete*, in which David's profile appeared, hit newsstands on May 10. Ten days later, news broke that David had recently undergone open-heart surgery to repair a freshly discovered congenital defect, a hole that had limited the organ's function to a fraction of normal capacity. Turned out everything he had ever done—BUD/S, Ranger School, overseas missions, Badwater, Ultraman—he'd done literally with half a heart.

THREE STEPS TO ADDRESSING REALITY

Addressing the reality of a bad situation means making the best of it. As we've learned, to do so you must first accept the reality (i.e., recognize it as bad in a way that preserves your ability to make choices), and then embrace it (i.e., commit to making the best of it). But accepting and embracing the reality of a bad situation are no guarantee that you will address it. Put another way, even after you've accepted that life has given you lemons and decided to make lemonade from them, you still have to make the damn lemonade.

For my money, no athlete models this third step more helpfully than David Goggins. But, like anyone else, he had to complete the first two steps to even reach the third, and it wasn't easy. David's whole life has been bad situations, in part because he seeks them out. There is, however, one bad situation he didn't choose—his awful childhood—and it was this particular reality that David needed to accept and embrace before he could properly address it.

In his 2018 memoir *Can't Hurt Me*, David describes a personal crisis that occurred between his second and third attempts to complete SEAL training, when he was back in Indiana nursing his fractured kneecap. Discouraged, deeply in debt, stuck in an unhappy marriage, and having just found out he was going to be a father, he began to doubt his desire to become a SEAL. It all came to a head one night on his mother's couch when he realized that he was ruled by fear, a fear rooted in those naked belt whippings of his youth, and that only by accepting this truth and embracing it as his real mission to overcome this fear would he be set free to become who he really was.

"All my fears came from that deep-seated uneasiness I carried with being David Goggins because of what I'd gone through," he writes. "Right there on mom's couch, as the moon burned its arc in the night sky, I faced down my demons. I faced myself. I couldn't run from my dad anymore. I had to accept that he was part of me."

For many years before this night of soul-searching, driven by gut instinct, David had endeavored to achieve complete mastery of his mind by pushing back the limits of his capacity to suffer until those limits disappeared. But he hadn't yet succeeded. On his mother's couch, at age 27, David finally accepted the true nature of the problem he was trying to solve: fear and self-rejection. These were the lemons life had given him, his underlying bad situation. The only solution was to neutralize once and for all his father's power to hurt him by attaining self-acceptance. That's what it meant to make lemonade. Now all he had to do was embrace this solution by resuming the quest to master his mind through voluntary suffering, knowing now what the fight was actually for, and this time he succeeded.

Let's now talk about the process by which David Goggins succeeded in addressing the reality of his bad situation, and how others do the same. Three things are needed to address a bad situation you've accepted and embraced:

1) The what
2) The why
3) The how

As you will soon see, these three things are interrelated, and each demands a deep engagement with reality.

The What: A Goal

"I should have been a statistic," David Goggins likes to say. Well, Chris Wilson *was* a statistic before he made an astonishing personal comeback that's described in his autobiography, *The Master Plan*. Although Chris is not an athlete, his story is a virtual blueprint for making the best of a bad situation, a useful model for athletes and nonathletes alike.

Born in 1977, Chris had the dual misfortune of being the child of a single mother who became addicted to drugs and attached herself to a series of no-good men and of reaching adolescence in the poverty-ridden Baltimore area at the height of the crack epidemic. Like everyone around him, Chris did what he felt he had to do to survive, and what he felt he had to do, unfortunately, was carry a gun and use it on one of two strange men who threatened him on a dark street one night when he was 16 years old. The outcome of this terrible but almost inevitable mistake was a life sentence in prison without the possibility of parole.

Chris's first year inside was a total waste. Seeing no future, he descended into a state of apathy so absolute that he stopped combing his hair and shaving. But when he came under the influence of an older inmate who offered Chris a positive role model, he began to turn himself around, and over the next 15 years he earned his GED and an associate's degree; taught himself Italian, Spanish, and Mandarin; joined and later led the prison's inmate advisory council; started a profitable (profitable for the prison, that is) photography business as well as a number of self-improvement clubs for his fellow prisoners, including a book club and a real estate group; beat astronomical odds to earn a sentence reduction hearing, where he beat the odds a second time by prevailing; and, following his release, became a social entrepreneur, launching several businesses that employ men newly released from incarceration.

The first step Chris took in this transformation was to wake up early one morning and go for a run alone in the prison yard. That cleared his head. The next step was a simple question that Chris asked himself after deciding to move beyond apathy and try to make the best of his situation: *What's your end game?* Chris knew he didn't want to die behind bars, nor did he want to be as good as dead while he remained locked up, but what *did* he want? He spent several days answering this question on paper, calling the eventual result the Master Plan, which he revised many times in the ensuing years as he turned it step by step into reality.

When things go wrong, we often know what we don't want before we have a clear idea what we do want as an alternative to our present reality. For example, you might be halfway through a marathon and on pace to beat your goal time when your left calf begins to cramp, forcing you to slow down. Your immediate reaction may be to feel disappointment and wish the cramp weren't happening. That's only human. But to make the best of the situation, you must execute a psychological pivot from wishing to willing as quickly as possible, replacing your original goal with a substitute. In the case of a mid-marathon calf cramp, your best move is probably to challenge yourself to find and maintain the fastest pace that doesn't cause the muscle to seize up again.

Knowing your endgame in a bad situation is important for two reasons. One is that it reengages you in reality by shifting your attention from wishing what's happening weren't happening (denial of reality) to creating a reality you prefer. Coming up with a new goal also increases your chances of achieving an outcome you're satisfied with by defining for yourself what it means to make the best of your situation.

In some cases, as in the example I just gave, the most sensible substitute for your original goal is pretty obvious. In other cases, a variety of substitutes might present themselves, and it's up to you to choose the one that's right for you. Suppose you choke in an important race, becoming so overwhelmed by pressure to meet expectations that you severely underperform. No athlete wants to choke—that's a given. But what do you want to do instead? There are several possibilities. You could avoid future choking by lowering your expectations, or by taking a break from racing. Or you could challenge yourself to cowboy up, using the shame of your choking episode as fuel to propel you to success in your next race. Yet another option is to identify and address the root cause of your choking. Any one of these goals might be the right one for you at a given moment in your athletic life. The point is that the ball is in your court, the choice yours to make.

Recognizing the appropriate endgame for a particular bad situation requires an active effort, something more than just wishing things hadn't gone wrong, and it often demands extensive reflection. In this way, bad situations are opportunities to get real with yourself and decide what you *truly* want instead of persisting in the pursuit of superficial goals that may merely represent what you think you're supposed to want. Often, when things go wrong, your original goal goes out the window, and you need a new or fallback goal. Coming up with one is a lot easier if you have an underlying goal that codifies the kind of athlete (or person) you are or want to be—what you stand for.

David Goggins knows what he stands for. *I just wanted to leave everything I had out there on that course.* These words, spoken in answer to Chris Kostman's question about David's goal for the 2007 Badwater Ultramarathon, represent his goal for every race since his very first—or, more accurately, since the 81-mile mark of that 100-mile Badwater qualifier in San Diego, where, having no clue how he was going to complete the last 19 miles, David discovered that what he'd thought was his goal wasn't really. It's a goal that breaks almost every rule of goal setting, as encapsulated in the classic S.M.A.R.T. acronym (specific, measurable, attainable, relevant, time-based), but that doesn't matter, because it's perfect for him.

"I finally realized that this fight wasn't about Operation Red Wings or the families of the fallen," David writes of his epiphany at 81 miles. "None of that would help me run 19 more miles before 10:00 a.m. No, this run, Badwater, my desire to push myself to the brink of destruction, was about me. It was about how much I was willing to suffer, how much more I could take, and how much I had to give."

David did, of course, complete those remaining 19 miles, but it wasn't the finishing that gave him satisfaction. It was a moment that occurred an hour or so later, as he lay curled in the fetal position in his bathtub pissing blood while his wife made frantic calls to doctors and hospitals. "This last part," he writes in his memoir. "This pain and suffering. This was my trophy ceremony."

If you look closely at the YouTube video I described earlier, you will notice that David doesn't smile when a finisher's medal is draped around his neck, a smattering of unseen spectators applauding the ceremony. But the ghost of a smile does appear seconds later, when Kostman asks him how he's feeling and David answers, "I have nothing left."

Goal achieved.

The Why: Motivation, Commitment

There comes a moment in almost every endurance race when we ask ourselves, "Why am I doing this?" It's our mind's way of checking in with our soul to determine whether continuing to push toward the finish line is worth our present suffering, not to mention the pain to come. David Goggins offers some advice on handling these moments in *Can't Hurt Me*: "Once you're in the heat of battle, it comes down to staying power. If it's a difficult physical challenge, you will probably have to defeat your own demons before you can take your opponent's soul. That means rehearsing answers to the simple question that is sure to rise up like a thought bubble: 'Why am I here?' If you know that moment is coming and have your answer ready, you will be equipped to make the split-second decision to ignore your weakened mind and keep moving. Know why you're in the fight to stay in the fight!"

Implicit in this counsel is the idea that individual athletes have different reasons for racing. Not every reason for racing is equally effective as an incentive for staying in the fight, however. Consider the following hypothetical answers to the question, "Why am I here?"

> Because I want to impress Jim, a runner I'm interested in dating.
> Because I want to set an example of strength and determination for my children, and if I quit, I will feel I have failed in my role as a parent, which is the single most important part of my life.

Clearly, the second reason will act as a more potent incentive to keep the athlete going. As a general rule, the higher the perceived stakes of racing are, the closer the athlete will come to giving a 100 percent effort. For David, life is essentially a long series of naked belt whippings, and the way to survive it is to "callus the mind" to suffering. He runs ultramarathons not because he loves running but because it is one of the best ways to callus the mind, but only to the extent that he suffers in pursuit of the finish line. Those are some pretty high stakes, and they are why David has been able to do such things as run 100 miles on zero training.

Psychologists refer to the phenomenon in question as *motivational intensity*. Developed by Jack Brehm in the 1980s, motivational intensity theory is a general theory of human motivation that has recently been applied to sports, most notably in Samuele Marcora's psychobiological model of endurance performance. Brehm's theory posits that individuals enter into difficult tasks with a certain degree of potential motivation that predetermines the maximal amount of effort they are willing to exert in order to achieve their goal. If this limit is reached before the goal has been achieved, they disengage. Marcora has argued—and proven, through cleverly designed experiments—that endurance racing is like any other task in that, when an athlete quits a race or hits the wall, it is not because the body has encountered a hard physical limit but rather because the athlete has decided, consciously or not, that the effort required to keep pushing is too great. Hard physical limits do exist, but they are never reached (except in special cases, such as heat exhaustion) because one of two things always happens first: the goal is achieved or the effort required to continue pursuing the goal exceeds the athlete's motivation and the athlete backs off.

What makes endurance racing tricky is that you never know exactly how much suffering will be required to succeed until you are confronted with the reality of it. Athletes who take David Goggins's advice and rehearse their answer to the "Why am I here?" question will certainly be more prepared than others to face this reality, but whether their answer supplies enough potential motivation to overcome the suffering remains to be seen until they reach the moment of peak effort. Every athlete assumes their reason for racing will suffice to power them to their goal—otherwise they wouldn't bother to start—but athletes with high-stakes motivations like setting an example for their children are a lot more likely to be right in this belief than are those with shallower motivations like impressing a potential date. In this sense, athletes who formulate motivations that connect racing to their deepest values are being more real with themselves, seldom if ever being forced to admit as they throw in the towel, "I guess I didn't want it as badly as I thought."

Interestingly, David Goggins himself doesn't believe in motivation. "Motivation changes exactly nobody," he writes in his memoir. "Even the best pep talk or self-help hack is nothing but a temporary fix. It won't rewire your brain." For David, "rewiring the brain" means "callusing the mind" to suffering, and it takes a lot of hard work, not a lot of motivation, to do that. On this point, David and I disagree. For where does the willingness to work hard come from? That's right: motivation!

Consider the lengths to which people who are addicted to drugs will go to obtain their substance of abuse. In the quest for the next fix, many addicts demonstrate a doggedness, a resourcefulness, and a willingness to take risks that few endurance athletes can equal in their pursuit of competitive goals. Do these folks have callused minds? Perhaps some of them do. But recent findings in the field of neuropsychology show that addictive substances work by hijacking the brain's motivational machinery. The only real difference between an addict's brain and yours or mine is what it wants and how badly it wants it.

There's no question that certain psychological factors other than motivation, such as willpower, contribute to the capacity to suffer in pursuit of goals. In true life-or-death situations, everyone's motivation is more or less equal, and yet some individuals—perhaps those with more callused minds—will fight harder for their lives than others will. In everyday life, though (which includes the sporting context), it all starts with motivation. If you want it badly enough, you will cultivate those other factors over time.

So that's one half of the *why* of addressing reality. The other half, closely related, is commitment. Motivation is the desire to do something; commitment is a pledge to do something that may or may not have an underlying motivation. Although it is easier to commit to an action you genuinely want to undertake, you can commit to doing things you don't really want to do, and motivation without commitment won't take you very far. In other words, the effects of motivation and commitment on the effort to address reality are additive.

In real-world practice, a commitment is not so much a technique used to get things done as a symbol and reinforcer of a person's intent to get something done. When people are truly serious about adhering to a certain intention, they tend naturally to make an explicit commitment. For example, whereas a person who's not so serious about losing weight might think, *Tomorrow I'm going to start trying to lose some weight*, a person who's serious is more likely to think, *Starting today, I'm going to increase my vegetable intake to three servings a day, walk two miles every morning, and reduce my wine consumption to one glass a day.*

Among athletes, commitment distinguishes finishers from quitters. This was shown in a 2018 study led by Karine Corrion of the University of the French Riviera and published in *PLoS One*. More than 200 runners completed a survey that extracted information on motivation, planned behavior, and coping strategies prior to competing in a 140 km trail race. Among the variables the survey measured was intention to finish the race. You might be thinking: *Who starts a 140 km trail ultramarathon without intending to finish?*

But there are many degrees of intention to finish, ranging from a tacit hope that everything works out (weak intention) to an explicit commitment to cross the finish line no matter what (strong intention). Corrion's subjects were asked to rate the strength of their intention to finish using a five-point scale. As it turned out, the attrition rate was high, with only 96 subjects (43 percent) going the distance. The average intention-to-finish score within this subgroup was 4.34, compared to 3.07 among non-finishers. This made intention to finish (i.e., commitment) the second strongest psychological predictor of a successful finish after self-efficacy.

Perhaps the simplest way to commit to a goal is to adopt a *no-excuses mentality*. This entails telling yourself explicitly that you will do what you intend to do come hell or high water. A good example of how the no-excuses mentality is used in sports is the run-streak phenomenon. Runners who choose to maintain a run streak commit to run every day (the United States Run Streaking Association requires at least a mile for official recognition) no matter what. Runners who make this commitment invariably discover that in the past they were fooling themselves when they decided to skip a planned run on a given day because it just wasn't possible. It was.

In 2019, I wrote an article on run streaking. Among the runners I interviewed was Tim Osberg, who had a seven-year streak going at the time and had previously seen a 26-year streak end on doctor's orders when he had a hernia operation. During that first streak, Tim shoveled his driveway in the midst of a blizzard so he could complete his daily run in tiny back-and-forth segments. Before the streak, he would have convinced himself that, with the streets and sidewalks being impassable, running just wasn't possible that day.

Chris Wilson regarded his Master Plan as one big no-excuses commitment. ("I had to complete every step, even the ones I hated," he writes.) Two years before his scheduled release from prison, Chris was moved to a halfway house in Baltimore, where a cruel and jealous caseworker thwarted him at every turn, first reducing his allowance of time outside the house as punishment for bringing home a good report card from the University of Baltimore, then withholding a pass to attend his mother's funeral, and finally sending him back to prison, and not just back to prison but to the mental health ward, a house of horrors that was crammed with inmates who defecated on themselves and screamed day and night and that was so filthy, prison guards put hazmat suits on before entering. There Chris continued his studies.

"I pulled the sheet off my bunk, sat on the floor, and wrapped it around my body like a cocoon," he recounts. "That's how I read, because it was the only way to keep off the flies. I wrote a term paper in that cocoon, in pencil, scrawling on the front and back and all the way to the edges because I had a limited supply of paper. I could feel the roaches crawling . . . I wasn't going to pass that class, obviously. I couldn't even turn in my paper. But that didn't matter. What mattered was the work."

The message here is not that everyone should go to any length to achieve every goal. It is, rather, that it's important to be real with yourself when you're in a bad situation. Anything that stands in the way of achieving the outcome you desire in such a situation is either a *reason* or an *excuse*. Reasons for falling short of a goal include conscious choice (i.e., you voluntarily give less than a 100 percent effort) and factors beyond your control. Excuses are factors within your control that you deny by blaming something else. It's easy to conflate the two—specifically to think that an excuse for failure is not an excuse but a reason—and people do it all the time. As David Goggins writes, "Believe it or not, most people prefer delusion. They blame others or chaotic circumstance."

Not wanting a desired outcome badly enough to do everything possible to achieve it is a perfectly legitimate reason for falling short, but if it is the reason, admit it to yourself. Doing so not only shows character but it will also train your mind to accept reality generally, which will help you make the very best of the next bad situation that matters more to you.

The How: Improvisation, Belief

Boxer Mike Tyson famously said, "Everyone has a plan until they get punched in the mouth." While athletes in noncombat sports don't often get punched in the mouth, they do often see things go wrong in unexpected ways that force them to abandon their plan and improvise, or scramble, as I like to say. In golf, scrambling is the improvisational style of play that becomes necessary when you hit an errant tee shot and the ball ends up in the kind of lie you can't really practice for. Making the best of a bad situation requires that you scramble effectively. But how is this done? The answer that we get by studying the ultrarealists can be summed up in the familiar cliché, "Where there's a will, there's a way."

Some people are natural planners. Being one will put you in good stead when things are going your way. But when they're not, it's better to be highly motivated because desperation breeds resourcefulness (as we see with many addicts), and when you find yourself in a bad situation that you really want to make the best of, you feel desperate. In fact, being a natural planner can be a detriment when things go wrong because many planners loathe uncertainty, whereas scramblers are able to tackle a crisis with the attitude that they can figure out how to make the best of the situation as they go and that the important thing for now is to stay in the fight.

Chris Wilson is not a natural planner. He hadn't thought more than one step ahead in his entire life until he found himself locked up and desperate to change his reality. Simply asking himself the question, "What's my endgame?" was an awakening for him, a mental paradigm shift. Even then, the first iterations of his Master Plan were woefully shortsighted, rife with superficial ambitions such as joining the Mile High Club and partying on a cigarette boat. Over time, though, the Master Plan evolved in the direction of greater maturity, Chris's shallower objectives giving way to goals of self-improvement (one of which was to run a marathon), proving himself to the powers in whose hands his fate lay, and helping others. Because he had the will, he found a way.

David Goggins isn't a natural planner either. Heck, he did a 100-mile running event three days after he first conceived the idea of running 100 miles! Of course, he paid a heavy price for his lack of preparation. But because of (not despite) the suffering he endured in that experience, David came away from it highly motivated to see how far he could push himself as an ultrarunner, and he planned meticulously for his next race, Badwater, scouting the 135-mile course by car and marking the best locations for his support crew to stop and ply him with drinks, food, and ice, and even mapping the gas stations and convenience stores where these supplies could be obtained.

David's quest to break the world record for the most pull-ups completed in 24 hours followed a similar pattern. The goal itself was a scrambling response to his heart condition, which required two surgeries and prolonged recovery, and left David unable to run more than a couple of miles without experiencing dizzy spells even after his recovery was supposedly complete. "When an activity or exercise that you've always relied on gets taken away from you, like running was for me, it's easy to get stuck in a mental rut and stop doing any exercise at all," he writes in *Can't Hurt Me*, "but I didn't have a quitter's mentality. I gravitated toward the pull-up bar [because it] was an exercise that allowed me to push myself and didn't make me dizzy because I could take a break between sets."

His first record attempt took place live on *The Today Show*. Having done little more to prepare for the challenge than a ton of pull-ups, David fell humiliatingly far short of the number to beat (4,021). Chastened, he completed a full after action report (AAR), in which he identified a number of mistakes resulting from his lack of planning, not the least of which was using a bar provided by NBC that he hadn't properly tested. In his second attempt two months later, David not only used a better bar but also switched up his glove, fuel, and music selections and his cooling strategy—and he fell short again, this time by 800 reps. Another AAR, another two-month wait, and then a third try, this time with a more conservative pacing strategy that proved to be the difference-maker. David knocked out nine more reps than the previous record holder, who had a far better build for pull-ups than long-armed, thick-muscled David, much as Dean Karnazes has a better build for ultrarunning.

The second part of the *how* of turning athletic lemons into lemonade is belief. According to Brehm's motivational intensity theory, an effort level that exceeds a person's potential motivation is not the only factor that will cause that person to disengage from a goal-directed task. The other is the belief that the goal has fallen out of reach. Nobody in their right mind continues to pour effort into the pursuit of a goal that they truly believe is impossible to achieve. But what about when a goal seems *almost* impossible but not quite?

It is well established that risk appetite varies between individuals. Some folks are willing to spend a significant percentage of their income on lottery tickets; others aren't. Games of chance like lotteries are pure tests of risk appetite, but in sports and work and relationships and most areas of life, where a person has some control over the outcome, risk appetite gets mixed up with other psychological ingredients, including self-efficacy and optimism. The upshot is that in situations where achieving a goal is almost but not quite impossible, some people feel that going for it is worth the risk, while others do not.

Consider Lloyd Christmas, Jim Carrey's character in the film *Dumb and Dumber*. In one scene, Lloyd asks the woman he fancies what the chances arc of the two of them ending up together, and her answer is devastating: "One out of a million." Except Lloyd isn't devastated; he's ecstatic, grinning boyishly and gushing, "So you're telling me there's a chance!"

Now consider Eliud Kipchoge, whose coach, Patrick Sang, said the following about him after his first attempt to run a sub-two-hour marathon, something that experts gave him about a one in a million chance of achieving: "I did not know the capacity of the human mind until Eliud's first attempt to break the two-hour barrier at the Nike Breaking2 project. I knew the mind is strong, but I didn't realize how strong. On that morning,

I looked into his eyes, and he actually believed 100 percent that he was going to do it. Now, that did not happen in Monza, but he came so close, closer than many, many people expected. It was then that I realized how important belief is. Someone might believe they can do it, but do they truly believe? Is it just an 80 percent belief? With Eliud it is 100 percent."

Chris Wilson and David Goggins are wired similarly. Chris's fellow inmates told him he was wasting his time trying to get his life sentence reduced, but he tried anyway and succeeded. Few in the ultrarunning community gave David any chance of making it back to the top of the sport after his heart procedure and the slow comeback that ensued (not to mention his detour into chasing pull-up records). In 2016, after his retirement from the SEALs, he won three ultras, and in the same week his memoir was released, aged 43, he placed fifth in a highly competitive 50K.

In Chapter 3 we discussed the importance of perceiving reality accurately. But two people can perceive the same reality with equal accuracy and yet interpret it very differently. Optimists look at a 12-ounce glass containing 6 ounces of water and see a glass half full, pessimists a glass half empty. Same reality, different interpretations. Similarly, ultrarealists look at one-in-a-million odds and focus on the one, whereas most focus on the million. It's not that ultrarealists are bad at math; they just believe in their ability to be the one.

If you currently lack the ultrarealist attitude toward long odds and you'd like to acquire it, one way to do so is by selectively pursuing goals that you have a small but nonzero chance of achieving. For example, set a goal for your next 10K road race that you believe you have about a 10 percent chance of attaining. Prepare for this goal as assiduously as Eliud Kipchoge prepared for Breaking2, and then just go for it! If your calculations were correct, you will probably fall short, but you will not have failed because the experience will shift your mindset toward future challenges. You may not ever beat longer odds in your journey than David Goggins and Chris Wilson did in theirs, but I won't be the one to tell you that you can't.

2 MONTHS TO SANTA ROSA

I've been swimming with one arm lately. This is not by choice. An apparent muscle strain on the left side of my chest has left me temporarily unable to raise my left arm overhead without significant pain, and if you can't lift your arm overhead without significant pain, you sure as hell can't swim with it.

Scratch that. In fact, I *do* have a choice. Instead of swimming with one arm, I might swim with both arms and just put up with the pain, or I might decide not to swim at all. Thinking like an ultrarealist these past several months has taught me to always perceive choices. When things go wrong, it's easy to see yourself as a helpless puppet of fate, but I've come to recognize that this is never really true. A hundred different athletes in the same bad situation will not all deal with it the same way. Some of them will regard themselves as the puppeteer, not the puppet, and I'm trying to be that athlete in my present situation.

The injury occurred three days ago. I was having a really good swim, the technique work I've done with Mandy finally starting to pay off as I worked my way through a main set of seven times 200 yards descending. During the second interval, I felt a sudden and intense stinging sensation in my left pectorals, followed by a slowly radiating heat. It might have been wise to stop right away, but I talked myself into continuing on the grounds that I really needed to seize this opportunity to groove my improved stroke and that I could always stop later in the workout if the pain worsened. Well, the pain did worsen, but not a lot, so I settled on the compromise solution of completing the session and then resting my left arm until the injury heals.

I had a lesson with Mandy the next day, but I never do much actual swimming in these sessions, and I got through it without exacerbating the issue. Yesterday I improvised my own workout consisting of drills, kick sets, and one-arm swimming. After 800 yards, I was exhausted. But just 24 hours later, today, I managed 1,200 yards. Somehow, within this short span, my kick has become more efficient, generating greater power with less energy. Tomorrow I'll be back again, aiming to further reduce my best time for 50 yards with a kickboard.

I'm looking at this latest wrong turn as more of an opportunity than a setback. I've been reflecting on that chestnut from Marcus Aurelius: "The impediment to action advances action. What stands in the way becomes the way." A single reading of these words does not reveal the full depth of their profundity. Their author was not merely stating the obvious—that, if an obstacle seems to block the path toward your goal, you have no choice but to deal with it. He's saying that, if you have the right attitude, the obstacle in front of you is the very thing you need to advance toward your goal.

For the ultrarealist, it is a matter of indifference whether the path ahead is free of obstacles or filled with obstacles because all that matters—if you're the puppeteer and not the puppet—is that you know the material you must work with to get where you want to go. An unforeseen challenge is good news to no lesser degree than a surprise breakthrough is good news because both serve as useful guideposts to the next step. Both are material to work with, material chosen by forces beyond your control, so what point is there in having an opinion about which other material you might have preferred?

Am I glad that I strained a muscle three days ago? I am not. But I truly believe it will work out for the best. Adapting to my present inability to use my left arm affords me the opportunity to work on my kick, which has always sucked, and to concentrate on my weaker right arm stroke, and to put more effort into the drills Mandy has taught me. When I'm healthy, I tend to neglect these. Now that they're all I've got, they're getting the attention they deserve.

Ironman Santa Rosa is less than two months away. I hope and expect to be swimming normally again within a few days. It's possible, however, that the injury will heal slower than I expect, forcing me to continue swimming without my left arm for another week or two. Another possibility is that I return to full-bore swimming within a few days only to suffer a recurrence of the injury that relegates me to one-arm swimming even closer to race day. I will do everything in my power to prevent these scenarios from eventuating, but if either of them does, it will just be the next impediment to advance the action.

Come to think of it, there's an option between swimming without my left arm and swimming full-bore with it, which is using it very gently. Indeed, it occurs to me now that when I had my big breakthrough moment in the pool in 2003, it happened while I was swimming in slow motion, something my coach had suggested I do as a way to magnify the cost of my poor body position (that cost being sinking) and force my neuromuscular system to get creative in seeking ways to stay on top of the water. I can't wait to try it again!

6

COMING BACK
FROM A BAD BREAK

There is only one thing that I dread: not to be worthy of my sufferings.

FYODOR DOSTOEVSKY

BRAZILIAN RUNNER VANDERLEI DE LIMA held a commanding lead of 28 seconds over Stefano Baldini of Italy at the 35-kilometer mark of the 2004 Olympic Marathon in Athens when an insane Irish priest dressed like a kilted leprechaun dashed into the street and dragged the defenseless 119-pound runner off the course. Despite losing 15 seconds to the assault, Vanderlei quickly regained his composure and held on to claim the bronze medal.

As this bizarre incident illustrates, bad situations in endurance sports can come in infinite varieties. Yet each belongs to one of only three basic types: the bad break, the rude awakening, and self-sabotage. At a strategic level, the key to making the best of a bad situation is always the same, no matter the type: facing reality. At the tactical level, however, the process of facing reality looks a little different in each type of bad situation.

To draw an analogy, whereas the broad principles of injury prevention apply to all types of injury, the specific measures you might take to address a susceptibility to, say, bone injuries are different from those you might take to address a vulnerability to tendon injuries. Similarly, whereas accepting, embracing, and addressing reality are the required steps to overcome any bad situation you may encounter as an athlete, different tools are more useful than others in executing these three steps depending on whether you're coming back from a bad break, a rude awakening, or self-sabotage.

Of the three basic types of bad situations, the bad break is the one that generates most of the best-known stories. Examples include Emil Zátopek's comeback from food poisoning and a multiday hospitalization to win the 1950 European Championships 5000m and 10,000m, Greg LeMond's comeback from a near-fatal hunting accident to win the 1989 Tour de France with buckshot still lodged deep inside his body, and Chris Legh's comeback from a potentially fatal case of intestinal necrosis incurred during the 1997 Ironman World Championship to win two Ironmans and seven Ironman 70.3s. Any one of these stories might serve as a suitable vehicle for exploring the specifics of what it takes to come back from a bad break. In this chapter, however, I will examine a case that is less celebrated, yet equally inspiring and edifying.

In February 2019 I gave a talk on mental fitness to a group of triathletes at a training studio in Sacramento. When the event wrapped up, I hung around for a while drinking wine and chatting with a few of the attendees. Among them was an athlete in his early forties who introduced himself as Courtney Cardenas, and who told me that if I enjoyed sharing comeback stories as much as I claimed to, then I needed to write about his ex-wife, Jamie Whitmore.

It was not an unfamiliar name. In fact, I even remembered her nom de guerre: J-Dawg. Fifteen years before, I was among the many triathlon fans around the world captivated by Jamie's intense rivalry with fellow professional off-road triathlete Melanie McQuaid, a clash of peerless equals that ended all too abruptly when Jamie was diagnosed with a rare and particularly cruel form of cancer in 2008. But I didn't know the rest of the story, and the rest of the story, Courtney insisted—the comeback—was the reason I needed to write about her.

Several months passed before I got the opportunity to hear the full story from Jamie herself. We met at a coffeehouse near her home in Somerset, California, an unincorporated community nestled in the lush hills east of her native Sacramento. Running late, she burst through the door as if she had a score to settle, caught my wave, and limped confidently over to where I sat, her knee-length shorts exposing a sleeve-like black brace that is a permanent feature of her surgically ravaged left leg. We shook hands and approached the counter, where Jamie ordered a white mocha with whipped cream and I requested a cold brew. Judging the interior of the establishment too noisy for recording, we took our drinks outside to a music-free patio seating area to chat.

I had done some research and knew most of the facts of Jamie's postcancer comeback, but I knew little about the psychology that made it possible, beyond what I'd gotten from her ex-husband's perspective.

"Courtney described you as a beast," I said when we were settled in our seats. "What do you think he meant by that?"

Jamie laughed, evidently knowing exactly what he meant.

"My dad says I came out of the womb headstrong," she said.

Jamie has almost no memory of her parents as a couple. They were already divorced when, at the age of 4, she demanded swim lessons, wanting to be like her sister, Trina, who was six years older and a member of the swim team. Both girls spent the majority of their time with their mother, but Jamie was closer to her dad, who loved sports and had a competitive streak. Games and contests were the order of the day in the Whitmore home, and Jamie was determined to win them all: UNO, thumb wars, you name it.

Within a year of starting lessons at the local YMCA, Jamie had mastered all four strokes and was allowed to join Trina on the swim team. It was *almost* everything Jamie hoped it would be. She loved the training, the racing, the camaraderie, and her steady improvement. There was just one thing she didn't love: the coach, who did a lot of yelling—far too much for Jamie's taste. After putting up with him for several years, she decided she'd had enough and quit.

Already Jamie dreamed of becoming a professional athlete. All she needed was a sport. She played three years of softball, dabbled in volleyball with her father in a church league, and allowed some eighth-grade friends to talk her into running track. As with swimming, she was good but not great at all of these sports. Nevertheless, she remained confident she would find her niche eventually.

In the fall of 1989, Jamie enrolled at Valley High School in south Sacramento. The following spring, she was faced with a choice between swimming, volleyball, and track. It so happened that Jamie's freshman geometry teacher was also the school's track coach, and he pestered her almost daily to come out for the team until he wore her down. It was a decision she would not regret, performing well enough right out of the gate that no further persuasion was required to convince Jamie to drop other sports and focus exclusively on running for the next three years. As a junior, she finished 15th in the California state high school cross country championship, and the college recruiters came calling, a wooing process that ended with Jamie accepting a scholarship offer from Cal State Northridge.

Jamie's success continued there. As a freshman she recorded the third-fastest time for 10,000 meters in school history. But she got a little greedy, increasing her mileage too quickly and developing plantar fasciitis, her first injury. Jamie took it in stride, so to speak, focusing on what she could do (getting treatment from the university's sports medicine team, crosstraining) rather than on what she couldn't. As a result, she was running again within six weeks and running better than ever soon thereafter, setting a new school record of 17:55.03 for 5000 meters indoors before she graduated in 1999.

The problem, though, was that the top female collegians were running two minutes faster for the same distance. A self-described realist, Jamie knew she would never become a professional runner. But her faith that she would eventually find a sport she could be among the very best at was undiminished, and this faith received some validation a few months later, when Jamie saw pro triathlete Barb Lindquist interviewed on television after she won the US national championship and was struck by Barb's admission that she didn't consider herself a very good runner. That got her thinking.

The next day, Jamie talked her dad into buying her a bike. Running, for her, was a checked box, and she had no doubt that her swimming would come back around with a little work, but it remained to be seen whether she could ride well enough to make a real go as a triathlete. She had a lot to learn—including how to fix a flat tire—and when Jamie flatted during an early training ride in Elk Grove, she was forced to haul the bike to a nearby shop, where her embarrassment at lacking the tools and skills to fix her own flat was compounded by her lack of money to pay the mechanic on duty to fix it for her. Lucky for her, that mechanic was none other than Courtney Cardenas, Jamie's future ex-husband, and he made the repair free of charge.

A mountain biker himself, Courtney persuaded Jamie to give off-road riding a try. Like many newbies, she found it to be an exercise in frustration, spending more time on the ground, it seemed, than pedaling, and before long she switched back to the road. Then winter hit, and Jamie discovered something she hated even more than falling off a mountain bike: riding into cold headwinds on the road. So she went back to the trails, determined to master the art of staying upright.

Courtney made a game of it, attaching point values to various screwups to incentivize clean riding. Touching one foot down cost you one point, two feet, two points. If you crashed but landed upright, you collected three points, and if you ate it completely, four points were added to your total. The ultimate shame, though, punished with five points, was walking a section. Such was Jamie's competitive nature that she preferred crashing to losing, and with this ride-or-die attitude, she improved so rapidly that in less than two months, she was outriding Courtney's buddies and eyeing a shot at becoming a pro mountain biker.

She completed her first race in the spring of 2001, acquitting herself well enough to advance from the beginner category to the sport category for the next race, and by the end of the season, she had earned her pro license. Jamie hadn't given up on triathlon, however. When she learned that the XTERRA off-road triathlon series would host its US championship event in Lake Tahoe, Nevada, just a stone's throw from home, she marked her calendar. Jamie's professional mountain biking license allowed her to compete in the pro division, so she did, finishing second behind soon-to-be crowned world champion Anke Erlank of South Africa. But when it was discovered that Jamie also held an amateur license with USA Triathlon, which superseded the NORBA license and prohibited her from competing as a pro, she was disqualified.

Despite the Kafkaesque snafu, Jamie, now 24 years old, saw the way forward, and when she lined up for the XTERRA World Championship in Maui the following month, she did so as a duly accredited professional. Her sixth-place finish was less than she'd hoped for, but it got her a nibble of prize money and cemented her decision to commit to the full 2002 XTERRA series.

The following April, fortified by a winter of balanced training in all three triathlon disciplines, Jamie won the season opener in Saipan by nearly 11 minutes. It was the first of 37 XTERRA victories Jamie would amass over the next six years.

She didn't win everything, though, and when the series returned to Lake Tahoe for the 2002 US championship, Jamie found herself in a virtual tie for the series points lead with Melanie McQuaid, a Canadian up-and-comer who had a similar athletic background but a very different racing style. Three inches taller and 25 pounds heavier than Jamie, Melanie exploited a strong swim to establish an early lead, used raw power on the bike to extend that lead, and then just tried to hang on during the run, whereas Jamie played the cat to Melanie's mouse—always the hunter, never the hunted. As a non-American, Melanie did not stand in the way of Jamie's winning a national title, but whoever broke the tape would claim the series title and the $14,000 bonus that came with it.

True to precedent, Jamie staggered out of the frigid lake well behind Melanie, and the chase was on. The bike leg began with a 1,600-foot ascent on Tunnel Creek Road, a steep and sandy tire-spinner. Jamie did not so much as glimpse Melanie the whole way up, and it wasn't until she'd cleared the tree line on the Tahoe Rim Trail that she at last sighted the Canadian's pistoning form up ahead. Jamie mashed the pedals with redoubled force, determined to catch Melanie before her rival passed the 8,700-foot summit and gravity turned in her favor.

Driving herself as though this crucial vertex were not the approximate midpoint of the race but the finish line, Jamie latched on to Melanie's back wheel mere seconds before they got there, settled in briefly to gather herself, and surged ahead. The race was over before the run leg even started, Jamie cruising to her first of five national champion titles. The following month she arrived on Maui strongly favored to add a world championship victory to her résumé, a victory that, similar to the previous race, seemed a foregone conclusion when she reached the bike-run transition with more than a minute's lead on fellow American Candy Angle (Melanie was way back), only to discover that the event staff did not have her bag of running gear.

Video footage of the incident is instructive. Jamie becomes agitated, as any athlete would, but she doesn't panic. Instead, controlling what she can, she calls out her race number to aid the staff's search, resists berating them so that *they* don't panic, runs back out of the changing tent to double-check the racks where transition bags hang awaiting their owners, and removes her bike shoes, helmet, and backpack, so she's ready when the bag is produced.

Eighteen minutes later, while Jamie is playing catch-up on the run course, a local age-group athlete rolls into transition, discovers his bag missing as well, and has a complete meltdown, flying around the tent like a moth in a lampshade, screaming his race number incomprehensibly. And although Jamie wound up second, likely as a result of her contretemps, there can be no doubt whose race *experience* was more negatively impacted by the same bit of bad luck.

The following season saw Jamie and Melanie trading victories, with Jamie claiming the US championship and the series title at Lake Tahoe in September before finishing second to Melanie at the world championship in October. In 2004, same deal, right up to the series finale, but this time Jamie arrived on Maui with a new level of determination to break the pattern.

"This is the one race that's eluded me," she told a CBS Sports television interviewer on the eve of the world championship. "I want it bad."

The race began, as always, at Makena Beach on Maui's western coast. Jamie hated open-water swimming—especially the briny rough-water kind—and her only goal for the first leg was to survive. So instead of cozying up next to Melanie on the start line with the intent of shadowing her, she choose a swimmer closer to her own ability to draft off and was pleasantly surprised when she came out of the water between laps one and two of the 1500-meter swim and spotted Melanie's red-white-and-blue uniform ahead, about to plunge back into the surf.

Even greater encouragement awaited her at the swim-bike transition area, located in a grassy patch about a half-mile's run from shore, where Jamie, having gained back 7 of the 25 seconds she'd ceded to Melanie in the water, crossed paths with her rival as the latter wheeled her mountain bike toward the mount line. With practiced choreography, Jamie slipped off her swim shorts, exchanged her running shoes for bike shoes, donned fingerless gloves and a helmet, and raced after Melanie with a hand on the seat of her Felt RXC hardtail, its frame adorned with a photo of her 3-year-old corgi, Rikki, who had intestinal parasites and was being kept alive by an outrageously expensive medication that had strongly incentivized Jamie's nine victories in that season's XTERRA tour.

After a relatively tame 4-mile prologue, the bike course smacked racers in the face with a nasty, 1-mile, 1,200-foot climb up the lower slopes of the Haleakalā volcano, an ascent that bore the unoriginal but apposite name

Heartbreak Hill and that only the strongest riders in the field of 351 athletes could scale without dismounting. Melanie was one of them, and she soon took the lead of the women's race. Jamie, though also well capable of scaling the hill mounted, got bogged down at the base behind a zombie march of faster swimmers now out of their element and was forced to hop off her machine and push it up the mountain, threading between human obstacles.

The reward that racers got for summiting Heartbreak was a second, similar climb, and their reward for *that* was a bone-rattling ride down the Plunge, a treacherous drop back toward the sea. Already more than two minutes behind, Jamie made it all of 100 feet down the obstacle-strewn descent before careening off the trail and somersaulting into a shrub. Unfazed, she picked up her bike, remounted, and rode on, only to take a second tumble. By the time she reached bottom, Jamie was covered in dirt and scrapes and more than three minutes off the lead.

Attacking the start of the 5.3-mile run course at a speed she only hoped she could sustain for the required distance, Jamie gained confidence from spectator reports on Melanie's shrinking advantage. She passed her rival on another treacherous downslope, Melanie giving her adversary a sporting pat on the backside as Jamie barreled past, Jamie responding with a gasping "Good job."

Then came Jamie's turn to pay for her win-or-die-trying race tactics. Slack-cheeked, her arms hanging lifelessly at her sides, the sleeveless white top she wore now soaked red with henna bled from her braided pigtails, she blundered blindly across an ankle-twisting rock beach that served as the homestretch to the finish line at Wailea Marriott Resort, looking more like an escaped POW with a head wound straining to reach the safety of the border than like the world champion that she was about to be crowned. But when she broke the tape, the curse was lifted at last. And at 28, she could look forward to a long reign as the queen of XTERRA.

Except it didn't work out that way. The next year, battling a cold, Jamie swam slower, rode slower, ran slower, and took third place. In 2006, she crashed spectacularly on the Plunge and showed up at the awards dinner that night on crutches.

Yet her dominance continued everywhere else. In 2007, Jamie came to Maui having won yet another XTERRA series title and another XTERRA USA Championship title. She'd been injury-free since recovering from the previous year's crash and hadn't so much as sneezed in weeks. But just 3 miles into the bike course, Jamie felt a strange weakness in her left leg. On Heartbreak Hill, it began to cramp. Reminding herself that she had battled through pain to win other races, she pushed as hard as she could with a leg and a half, hoping the cramping would ease up on the run. Instead it got worse, becoming so painful Jamie was reduced to a shuffle, gutting her way to a third-place finish.

At the hotel that night Jamie was bothered by a tingling sensation that radiated all the way from the buttock to the calf. Having just completed her last race of the season, she decided to take a little time off from running, confident that whatever minor damage she'd done to herself would heal quickly with rest. But the troubling symptoms persisted. While playing Wii with her family at Christmas, she had to sit down between turns to alleviate discomfort around the sciatic nerve.

By late January, when Jamie attended a Christian triathlon camp in Phoenix, she'd tried running just twice, aborting both runs due to extreme tightness in the left hamstring. At the camp she tried again, and was again forced to bail, the tightness having migrated to her calf. Even worse, cycling hurt too now, and on the last night of the camp, a throbbing sensation that lingered from the day's big climb kept her awake until dawn. After five more days of rest, Jamie went for a gentle test spin near her home, but within 15 minutes she was in so much pain that she turned around and pedaled back to her car in tears.

Jamie began to experience numbness in her leg even at rest, especially when she used the bathroom, and she could no longer lie flat on her back, as it caused unbearable pain in her lower spine. When she reported these developments to a physician friend, he ordered her to go straight to the nearest emergency room and request a CT scan of her abdominal area. Harried by more obvious emergencies, the doctor assigned to her dismissed Jamie's case as likely nothing more than an aggravated sciatic nerve related to overuse. She'd spent six hours at the hospital and went home without a scan.

Jamie's physician friend urged her to try again somewhere else, ASAP, so Courtney drove her to a hospital 90 minutes away in Roseville, where she spent another several hours losing the triage competition to heart attack and accident victims. This time, though, she got her scan, which revealed a large mass that also showed up in a subsequent ultrasound. Informed that it was probably an ovarian cyst, Jamie was sent home with instructions to make an appointment with an OB-GYN.

A rectal exam done at that appointment yielded the discovery that the mass was too hard to be a cyst, which meant it was probably a tumor, and so, like a hot potato, Jamie was passed on to an ovarian cancer specialist. Up to this point, Jamie had kept her focus on the 2008 XTERRA season, whose kickoff event in Saipan was now just a few weeks away, intending to retreat from her planned racing schedule step by step as her medical situation stretched out. Her idea was to delay her season debut to South Africa, if need be, or Ogden, if that didn't work, or Lake Tahoe, in a pinch, or Maui as a very last resort. But hearing that word, *cancer*, knocked her thinking onto a different track. No longer did Jamie want her health back for racing's sake; she now wanted it back for health's sake.

The ovarian cancer specialist Jamie was referred to conducted a laparoscopy, a minimally invasive method of collecting a sample of the mass for testing, but during the procedure he sliced through a blood vessel and Jamie began to bleed out, so he cut her open for real and kept her overnight. Adding insult to injury, he was unable to extract a sample suitable for testing, so after she was released from the hospital, Jamie met with a second specialist, accompanied by both her husband and her father.

"This is a pretty big tumor," he told them, sounding more impressed than concerned. "Ten or 20 years ago, we would have just amputated your leg."

Jamie broke down in tears, and her father took over.

"What would you do if Jamie were your daughter?" he asked.

"I would get a second opinion," he said.

Jamie's next stop was UCSF Medical Center, where Jamie met with a nerve specialist. By the time she saw him she was in agony, unable to bend, straighten, or put weight on her left leg, which had begun to atrophy from disuse. It didn't take a nerve specialist to recognize the direness of her situation, and Jamie was immediately prescribed a cocktail of strong pain medications and scheduled for major surgery.

When she woke up in the recovery room, one of the surgeons who'd worked on her placed a hand on Jamie's left foot and asked her to wiggle her toes. She couldn't even feel the doctor's hand. That's when she got the news that in removing the tumor (a spindle cell sarcoma, it turned out), the surgical team had also removed her sciatic nerve, which in the best case would leave her with a severe and permanent case of drop foot, unable to walk without a brace and certainly unable to run again.

Ever the realist, Jamie understood full well that running without a sciatic nerve would be about as likely as growing back an amputated limb. But whether she ran or not, she vowed that she would be an athlete again, in any way possible. "I want to feel the wind blowing in my face and my heart rate skyrocket when I am attempting a difficult section," she wrote in her blog. "I want to feel the endorphins from running 10 miles at a steady pace."

She got started on her comeback—wherever it might lead—right away, creeping up and down the hospital ward halls with her walker until she'd practically worn a rut in the tiles, progressing so rapidly that she was released after a few days. At home, she walked every day and hired a physical therapist to work with her once a week. By the time she started radiation therapy in June, she was also swimming 3,000 yards daily and lifting weights every other day. But no sooner had she gotten some momentum going than Jamie was informed that her tumor had grown back and a second operation was needed. She continued radiation for another three weeks and then went back under the knife, this time losing most of her left gluteal muscle, her sacral nerve, and a chunk of her tailbone along with the tumor.

The twelve-and-a-half-hour surgery was followed by a 10-day confinement to a hospital bed, where Jamie lay in a state of effective paralysis, in near-constant pain, unable to eat or eliminate bodily waste on her own. She was sent home with a tube dangling from her midsection, the purpose of which was to drain fluid from her internal wounds and help prevent infection. It didn't work so well. The day after she got home, Jamie developed a fever and started throwing up. When her temperature hit 104 degrees, Courtney raced her back to the hospital, where she learned that she had sepsis, a life-threatening reaction to inflammation in vital organs.

Jamie remained in the hospital for two weeks, receiving all of her nutrition intravenously, her weight dropping to 98 pounds. On her second day back home, she started vomiting again. Off she went the hospital.

Bone infection. A pick line was inserted into Jamie's left arm to deliver antibiotics from a bag around the clock. She was allowed to go home, at least, where she came up with a way to attach the bag to her walker and walked with it, finding some consolation in her doctor's decision to cancel chemotherapy on account of the sepsis, a departure from the original plan that would allow her to accelerate her return to bike riding. The only remaining obstacle, after the bag's removal, was the nephrostomy tube that drained Jamie's left kidney, a tripping hazard that was nearly ripped out of her one day when it got caught in the rowing machine she was using. She got rid of it the proper way six months later, when she went in for one last surgery, in which her left kidney was autotransplanted to her right pelvic area, where it could share the other kidney's ureter.

It was now June 2009. The past 18 months had tested Jamie's spirit to the limit. "I tried to remain as positive as possible," she told writer Timothy

Carlson, "but it was becoming more and more difficult. When you keep getting beat down so hard and have no energy and you can't eat or keep fluids down, it's difficult to be positive all the time. I have never felt closer to God. I spent all my time praying to Him, asking for a better tomorrow. Could tomorrow be just a little better than today?"

Not quite. Days after she gave that interview, Jamie got sick again. This time the main symptoms were lack of energy, nausea, and abdominal discomfort. Fearful that her body was rejecting her own kidney, she went in for more tests, the results of which were delivered to her in just two words.

"You're pregnant."

"What!" Jamie exclaimed. *"How?"*

It wasn't that she didn't know the birds and the bees. Jamie had just sort of assumed she *couldn't* get pregnant, given all her body had gone through. Less than six months into her term, however, she went into premature labor. To fend off miscarriage, she was hospitalized yet again and placed on 24-hour bed rest for the next seven and a half weeks, until her twin boys Christian and Ryder were born healthy and whole.

Another year would pass before Jamie could ride a bike again. That's how long it took her to discover the Allard BlueROCKER—the only brace that was strong enough yet stiff enough to allow her to pedal with her disabled left leg (she shattered the first brace she tried). Back in the saddle at long last, Jamie got straight down to the business of erasing the bad taste left in her mouth by her last XTERRA (and her last race as an able-bodied athlete). In 2011, Jamie completed the XTERRA Pacific Championship in Santa Cruz, using crutches during the 5K run leg and winning the physically challenged division.

She had far greater ambitions. The Leadville Trail 100 MTB—yes, the same event Rob Krar did amidst his own comeback—had been on her bucket list for a long time, and in August 2012 she gave it a shot. Her goal was not just to finish but to earn one of the coveted belt buckles reserved for those who cover the distance in less than 12 hours. Jamie's longest training ride before the race was just 55 miles, and she accepted she was in for a hard day, yet figured that with a combination of smart pacing and sheer determination she could get through it.

By her own reckoning, Jamie's fellow racers probably couldn't tell she had a disability until about halfway up the long climb to Columbia Mine, the course's high point, where her weakened left leg raised a white flag, forcing Jamie to hop off her bike and proceed on foot. As helpful as it is for cycling, the BlueROCKER sucks for walking, but Jamie had no option other than to grind out the remaining 1.5 miles to the summit as best she could. When she reached the top, she paused to savor the view from nearly 13,000 feet, and wept, remembering her many long days trapped in a hospital bed, wondering if a moment like this would ever come.

"For me it was a greater accomplishment than anything I had ever done," Jamie told me seven years later. "I didn't do this as a pro. I beat cancer, I had kids, and I did this with a disability. You couldn't knock me off that mountaintop."

It wasn't over yet. Eighty-seven miles into the race, Jamie learned that the Leadville Trail 100 MTB was actually 104 miles, which meant an extra 15 to 20 minutes of riding, a bad-news bombshell for the exhausted athlete. She turned the cranks with desperate force, one eye on her chronometer, her hope of achieving her 12-hour time goal fading by the second. Vicious cramps in her overworked abdominal muscles balled them up like little tumors. But pain was nothing new to Jamie, and she held on to cross the line in 11:42:37 and claim her belt buckle.

Soon afterward Jamie was contacted by a representative of the US Paralympic Cycling Team, who sought to gauge her interest in competing against other disabled riders. She leapt at the opportunity, and in 2013 Jamie won world championship gold medals in the road race and the time trial. Persuaded to give track cycling a try, she broke two world records and won two gold medals on the track the following year while defending both road titles. Having added three more gold and two silver medals to her résumé in 2015, she arrived at the 2016 Paralympic Games in Rio as the woman to beat.

And she *was* beaten, taking silver in the individual pursuit, finishing well back in the 500-meter time trial, and coming home seventh in the road time trial, slowed by a misalignment of her front brake that created friction between it and her front tire. That left the road race as her last chance for glory. A weak sprinter, Jamie came to the start line of the 47.4-kilometer double out-and-back course determined not to let the race come down to the wire. She had to break away from her fellow competitors at some point, but this was easier said than done, as the course had only one small hill, which the field would climb twice in each direction.

Patient through the first lap, Jamie saved her big attack for the penultimate climb. Only Sini Zeng of China and Denise Schindler of Germany were able to go with her, and on the ensuing descent Jamie put all that mountain biking experience to use, taking a tight corner on wet pavement harder than her pursuers dared and opening a small gap.

With 5 km of ground left to cover, every centimeter of it straight into a stiff headwind, Jamie knew better than to ride herself into the ground in an effort to keep away. Still, she pushed hard enough to ensure that no one else besides Sini and Denise would catch her, and that they'd have to work for it. Hauled in with 2 km to go, Jamie accepted that the race was going to come down to the wire after all and resolved to compensate for her lack of sprint power with superior wits. Approaching the final bend on the course, Jamie drifted to the inside, giving herself the shortest route to the finish, then stood on the pedals and stomped like she was putting out a fire, nipping Sini at the line by a fraction of a second and becoming the first person ever to win a world championship as an able-bodied athlete in one endurance sport and a Paralympic gold medal in another.

HOW TO BE A BEAST

Jamie Whitmore's story is a virtual clinic in how to come back from a bad break. Four features of her comeback stand out as examples for others to follow. Three of them—controlling the controllable, being comfortable with uncertainty, and narrativizing—we've touched on in previous chapters, but are worth reviewing here in their specific application to coming back from a bad break. The other—non-entitlement—is new, and it is especially helpful as a tool for facing reality when a bad break has occurred.

1) Non-Entitlement

When things go wrong, many people ask, "Why me?" Ultrarealists don't. That's because the question is born of a sense of entitlement—of being too special a person for bad things to happen to. This mindset makes it difficult to accept the reality of a bad situation and almost impossible to make the best of it. Jamie doesn't like it when things go wrong any more than the rest of us do, but she does not consider it beneath her dignity to have to solve problems she didn't cause. Nor should any of us.

I asked Jamie whether winning as a disabled athlete meant as much to her as winning against the world's best able-bodied athletes once had. She said it did, and given what she had told me already about her experience of the Leadville Trail 100 MTB ("For me it was a greater accomplishment than anything I had ever done"), I believed her. As for her cancer battle, Jamie said between sips of her white mocha with whipped cream, "I would allow myself to feel sorry for my situation or be angry at it for 15 minutes a day. After that, it doesn't get you anywhere. Being mad is not going to make you a world champion." Or save your life.

2) A Focus on the Controllable

In a bad situation, it's easy to fixate on the problem you're facing, but it's far more helpful to give your attention to finding a solution. Consider again the disparate reactions of Jamie and the local age-grouper who came into the bike-run transition of the 2002 XTERRA World Championship facing the problem of missing gear bags. Fixating on the problem, he flew about the tent like a moth in a lampshade, which solved nothing, whereas Jamie adopted a solution focus, doing what little she could to help fix the problem.

"I've always been the type to say, 'What *can* I control?'" Jamie explained to me. "Even with cancer, it was, 'Well, what *can* I do?'" Because there's so much you can't do."

Thankfully, relatively few of us will ever have to go through the experience of having our bodies and athletic capabilities permanently altered by disease, but even in facing far more common problems, such as overuse injuries, a solution focus can make all the difference. Given a diagnosis of, say, plantar fasciitis, many runners will spend a lot of time brooding on their inability to run and do little more to solve the problem besides not run. When Jamie got this diagnosis, she sought treatment, threw herself into physical therapy, and crosstrained, thereby minimizing the injury's impact on her collegiate running career.

3) Being Comfortable with Uncertainty

It isn't always just pain or stress or disappointment that makes a bad situation bad. Often it's uncertainty too. When things aren't quite right and we don't know if, when, or how they can be made right, that uncertainty is itself a source of stress. But not all athletes are equally stressed out by this uncertainty.

If I had to describe Jamie Whitmore's mindset in four words, I would choose these: "I'll figure it out." She uttered the phrase several times during the 90 minutes we spent at the coffeehouse, and they characterize her handling of everything from her search for a sport in which she could truly excel to her quest to get back on a bike after her cancer diagnosis. "If someone tells me it's impossible, I refuse to believe there is not another way to do things," she told one interviewer when she was cancer-free but not yet riding again. "I told my dad, 'Maybe I will not be able to go from point A to point B in a straight line anymore. But I will still get from point A to point B.'"

Being stressed out by uncertainty is, to a large degree, a choice, not a necessity. It is to say, in essence, "Unless I know now exactly how I'm going to get from point A to point B, I'm going to assume I will *never* know." Ultrarealists don't distort reality in this way, and I encourage you to follow their example. If you don't know, just accept this uncertainty and concentrate on trying to figure it out.

4) Narrativizing

In Chapter 4, I mentioned that ultrarealists have a tendency to narrativize the trauma they experience, finding the good in it by reframing it as a meaningful episode in their personal journey. Jamie does this from a Christian perspective. "I believe there's purpose in everything I encounter," she told me. "There's purpose in my pain; there's purpose in my setbacks. Maybe someone is going to look at what I've gone through and what I've overcome and it's going to help them."

Using this tool is a matter of treating your life as a story of which you are the author, or at least a coauthor, with the power to transform what seems like an unhappy ending into just another chapter on the way to a happy ending. Despite all she's been through and all she's lost, Jamie truly believes she is living her happy ending. And why not? She chose it herself.

5 WEEKS TO SANTA ROSA

I am outside my comfort zone, and I don't like it. But I also like it. What I mean is, I like that I don't like it, if that makes any sense.

I'm testing a software tool from a company called INSCYD (pronounced *inside*) that helps endurance athletes identify ways to improve their fitness. Specifically, the tool takes cycling power data and uses it to indirectly measure different aspects of an athlete's bike fitness, including aerobic capacity (VO_2max) and anaerobic capacity (VLamax). A number of big-name endurance athletes, including Olympic and Ironman champion Jan Frodeno, use INSCYD to fine-tune their training and diet, and I figured if it's good enough for them, it's good enough for me.

A few weeks ago, I performed a sequence of bike tests that serve to generate the data that the software uses to assess cycling performance. They were pretty tough, but my bike training has been going well lately (the fitting and the insoles I got in November really did the trick with my knee), and I got through them okay. They comprised a 20-minute time trial that I had to start with a 60- to 90-second all-out effort, a 4-minute time trial starting the same way, and a handful of seated 15-second sprints in a high gear ratio. Greg from INSCYD emailed the results to me a couple of days later, and then phoned to discuss them and offer suggestions.

According to the software, my VO_2max is 62 ml/min/kg, which is about what you'd expect for an athlete of my performance level and age. My VLamax (a measure of the muscles' maximal rate of lactate production during very intense exercise) is 0.23 mmol/l/s, which is extremely low, but as Greg explained to me, a blunted anaerobic capacity is actually a good thing when you're training for a 99 percent aerobic event like an Ironman triathlon. Also good is my weight-adjusted anaerobic threshold power of 4.5 W/kg. The bottom line, Greg said, is that my overall cycling fitness is pretty much where it should be, and that my best opportunity to improve it before Ironman Santa Rosa is to increase my VO_2max.

This is easier said than done, because the most effective ways to increase aerobic capacity are to train a lot and to do regular high-intensity interval workouts, and I was already doing both before I was tested. Referring to these methods as "low-hanging fruit," Greg suggested I try a more sophisticated method that was shown to increase time to exhaustion at peak aerobic power in a group of triathletes in a 2017 study. And that's how I got out of my comfort zone.

Working out in the late afternoon is something I generally avoid. I like to have my last workout of the day done by 4:00 p.m. so I can enjoy a beer while doing a little writing before dinner. But the protocol Greg suggested requires that I perform a high-intensity interval workout on the bike in the late afternoon, as close as possible to dinnertime.

Another thing I try not to do unless I really have to is eat low-carb. My normal diet is centered on healthy, carbohydrate-rich foods such as potatoes and fruit, and I never crave carbs more than when I'm immersed in high-volume training, as I've been lately. But Greg's protocol requires that I eat a close-to-zero-carb dinner after completing the late-afternoon high-intensity interval ride.

My aversion to low-carb eating is nothing, however, compared to my aversion to running early in the morning, before breakfast. When I wake up, my first thought is food, every day without exception. A hearty breakfast at 5:15 a.m. leaves me ready to attack my first workout of the day around 9:00 a.m. But the third and final step of the protocol Greg suggested is a low-intensity run performed on an empty stomach soon after waking up.

Add the three parts together and you've got something close to an athletic root canal, from my perspective. But I trust the science, and I've been practicing the protocol once a week for the past four weeks. Late yesterday afternoon I did an 80-minute indoor ride featuring six 2-minute efforts at high intensity followed by a 10-minute transition run, for good measure. Then I ate a dinner of broiled salmon filets and steamed broccoli. No beer, no potatoes. This morning I got up at the usual time and immediately hopped on the treadmill and jogged for an hour while reading on my Kindle and listening to Spotify simultaneously to distract myself from my hunger.

Granola has never tasted as good as it did to me after I got off that treadmill. But you know what? I enjoyed everything that preceded it almost as much, to the exact degree that I didn't enjoy it. The regimen didn't feel good, but I felt good *about* doing it. Whether or not these weekly sorties outside my comfort zone increase my VO$_2$max, I feel they're already benefitting me in a different way.

There's something to be said for doing stuff that kind of sucks precisely because it kind of sucks. Endurance racing is extremely uncomfortable. To do it well, you must be comfortable being uncomfortable. If I choose to suffer only as much as necessary in training, I won't reach the same level of mental fitness I'll get to by embracing the suck of Greg's protocol, which is kind of like the exercise equivalent of taking cold showers—something you do to "put hair on your chest."

On race day, stuff will happen that I don't want to happen. More pain than I planned for, more suffering, misery, bad luck. Who's going to deal with these unwanted realities better: an athlete who trains hard but stays within his comfort zone or an athlete who trains hard and once a week chooses to do things he'd really rather not do? To me the answer is obvious, and I want to be the athlete who can handle the suck he didn't choose because he chose the suck he couldn't handle beforehand.

7

COMING BACK
FROM A RUDE AWAKENING

You're not trying to beat the Yankees or the Red Sox or the Blue Jays.
You're trying to beat the game of baseball through execution.
MAJOR LEAGUE BASEBALL MANAGER JOE MADDON

WHEN KATHERINE GRAINGER ARRIVED in Sydney in August 2000 for her first Olympics, she had zero expectations. Great Britain had never won an Olympic medal in a women's rowing event, so there was no standard for her quadruple sculls team to live up to. What's more, Katherine was the youngest, least experienced, and least accomplished member of the crew, a veritable parvenu.

She'd never even held an oar until seven years before, when she arrived at Edinburgh University as an 18-year-old aspiring law student. Having only the vaguest interest in sports generally, she was practically press-ganged into giving rowing a try by a member of the boat club who took note of Katherine's height (5′11″) at a freshers' week event. "I think you could be really good," the recruiter said.

She was right. After some initial flailing, Katherine improved rapidly, winning the prestigious Henley Royal Regatta on the River Thames in her third year at Edinburgh and earning captain status the following year. On graduating, she was offered the opportunity to try out for the British national team, eventually claiming the fourth and last slot on a boat that qualified for Sydney by winning the B final at the 1999 FISA World Championships.

Katherine soaked up the Olympic experience with childlike delight, mooning over the famous athletes she bumped into at the Village and soaking up the action occurring in other sports. When Australia's Cathy Freeman became the first indigenous person to claim Olympic gold in winning the women's 400 meters, Katherine was in the stands.

Lack of expectations notwithstanding, Katherine's boat qualified for the six-boat final, held on a torrid late-September morning on mirror-smooth water at Penrith Lakes. The primary emotions she felt before the start were excitement and a coltish eagerness to bolt that she fought to contain. Having recorded the fourth-fastest time in the heats, Katherine and her crewmates—Gillian Lindsay and sisters Guinn and Miriam Batten—intended to key off the Ukrainians (third-fastest time) during the race, judging this strategy their most likely path to the medal stand—both the German and the Russian boats being regarded as unbeatable. A good start put the Brits ahead of their rivals for bronze right away, and they stayed ahead for the full 2,000 meters, erupting in delirious celebration as they crossed the finish line.

There was a problem, however. No sooner had they docked than an official informed Katherine and her teammates that an announcement of the final results would be delayed for the examination of a photo finish. They were incredulous, knowing full well they'd beaten the Ukrainians by nearly two boat lengths. But the call to be made was not between Great Britain and Ukraine for third; it was between Russia and Great Britain for second.

In her autobiography, *Dreams Do Come True*, Katherine recalls of this moment, "I thought, 'Oh, no need for that. I'm over the moon with a medal. I don't mind what color it is.'" Yet, while officials studied the photo, Katherine continues, "I went from not caring to thinking, 'What a shame. It would have been nice if we had managed to pull off the silver,' to thinking, 'I'll actually be a bit disappointed if it's not silver now.' All in the space of

12 minutes. That is how fast expectations and standards can change." The decision came, and Katherine was not disappointed.

When she arrived in Athens in August 2004 for her second Olympics, Katherine had very high expectations. And why not? Not only had she won a silver medal at the previous Summer Games but she was also the reigning world champion, along with crewmate Cath Bishop, in the coxless pair. (It is not uncommon for elite rowers to switch events.) In a 2015 interview for the Olympic Channel, Katherine recalled, "We came in . . . knowing we had beaten everyone in the field, and therefore it's a different expectation. There was an expectation of, 'If we get this right, we will win the Olympic Games,' and that's a very different place to start from."

Whereas in 2000 she had marched proudly in the Opening Ceremony and had milked the Olympic Village experience for all it was worth, this time Katherine chose to skip the festivities and bed down at a location nearer the rowing venue at Schinias National Park. Despite her all-business mindset, Katherine and Cath laid an egg in their heat, finishing seven seconds behind Belarus and thus forced to contest the repechage (a last-chance qualifying race), which they won. In the final, the British pair were back on form, passing 500 meters just 0.69 seconds behind the leading Canadians. But not for long. An aggressive surge by the Romanian boat threw the race into chaos, leaving five teams scrambling for the lesser medals. With a desperate late burst, Katherine and Cath nipped the Belarusians at the line for silver, but it wasn't silver they'd come for.

On the dock, the Brits exhibited body language that contrasted sharply with Katherine's quad crew celebrations in Sydney, their smiles pinched, their back pats more commiserative than congratulatory. "It was a mixed medal," Katherine reflected in 2015. "If it was anything other than gold, it was going to be tinged with disappointment."

When Katherine arrived in Beijing in August 2008 for her third Olympics, her expectations were higher still. At a meeting of the British National Women's Rowing Team held in early winter 2005, a postmortem of the prior summer's Olympics was performed. All three British boats had medaled, yet none had won. So the team pledged that it was to be gold or nothing in China three years hence. For Katherine, this unforgiving standard became even more so as the Olympiad unfolded, Katherine winning three consecutive world championship titles in her new boat, a reconfigured quad that was named FISA's International Crew of the Year in 2007.

Conditions were good at Shunyi Olympic Rowing-Canoeing Park on the first day of racing. Competing in the first heat, the formidable British foursome laid down a marker, breaking the Olympic record for the 2,000-meter distance. That record stood for less than an hour, however, snatched away in the second heat by an upstart quad representing the host nation. In the final, Katherine's boat grabbed an early lead and held it all the way to the grandstands, where the Chinese unleashed a fierce attack, clawing ahead of the favorites to win by one second.

While the victors wept with joy, a funeral broke out on the runner-up boat. Katherine, in the stroke seat, shook her head in stunned disbelief, wondering what they'd done wrong, what they could do better next time. Then she remembered: There would be no next time, Katherine's plan having been to retire as an Olympic champion and turn her attention to completing her PhD studies in criminal law, forgoing the 2012 London Games.

All too soon a BBC microphone was thrust in Katherine's stricken face. Asked how it felt to get another silver medal she merely shrugged, mumbling a cliché about brides and bridesmaids. On the medal stand, all four members of the British crew wept openly. When Katherine was reunited with her family at the grandstands, she fell into her mother's consoling arms. Liz Grainger knew better than to remind her daughter that winning an Olympic silver medal wasn't such a bad thing, so instead she said just about the only thing that wouldn't have made the situation worse. "Promise me you'll be in London," she hissed in her daughter's ear. "You'll do it. I know you will."

WHEN IT'S HARDER THAN EXPECTED

Katherine Grainger's story (or what we've seen of it so far) is an object lesson in the power of expectations. Because of her evolving expectations,
each of the three silver medals she earned in her first three Olympics meant
something very different to her. As her career progressed and the successes
piled up, her expectations rose, and as her expectations rose, her satisfaction with silver decreased. This is neither a good thing nor a bad thing; it's
simply natural for highly competitive individuals like Katherine.

Psychologists have done some interesting research in the area of expectations. One study conducted by South Korean researchers Cecile Cho and
Theresa Cho and published in *Frontiers in Psychology* in 2018 compared the
effects of different expectation levels on subsequent disappointment. Con-
trary to what you might expect, subjects who set low expectations for the
outcome of a two-part test (part one being a proofreading exercise, part two
a simulated online investing game) were *more* likely to be disappointed in
the outcome, regardless of whether their goal was met.

This doesn't mean that setting high expectations eliminates the risk of
disappointment. Other research has shown that people are only ever consistently happy with outcomes when those outcomes are better than
expected, and the higher your expectations are, the harder it is to achieve a
better-than-expected outcome. What's more, psychologists have found that
expectations must in general be realistic to yield satisfaction, so if winning
an Olympic gold medal is a realistic expectation for you, you might as well
go with it, despite the inherent risk. In any case, disappointment isn't the
end of the world. As we'll see later in this chapter, an ultrarealist mindset
toward expectations can take the sting out of a disappointing outcome
while at the same time reducing the likelihood that such an outcome occurs
in the first place.

But what does any of this have to do with comebacks? Quite a bit. Among
the three major types of comeback that athletes commonly experience, one

is in fact all about expectations: the comeback from a rude awakening. Merriam-Webster defines a rude awakening as "a surprising and unpleasant discovery that one is mistaken." In sport, rude awakenings primarily take the form of harder-than-expected experiences, of which there is no shortage for most athletes. For starters, almost every race is harder than expected at some point. This is the case for two reasons. The first is that racing is inherently hard. If you ever complete a race without having felt like you were at your absolute limit, you weren't really racing.

The second reason races surprise us by how hard they are is that we have a natural tendency to remember aversive experiences as being less unpleasant than they were at the time. (A friend of mine with four children told me no woman in her right mind would choose to go through a second childbirth otherwise!) Repetition counteracts this tendency to a degree, but even experienced athletes tend to forget how painful the last race was by the time they start the next race and thus get a rude awakening when they find themselves back in that place.

On a broader timescale, athletes often find it harder than expected to achieve goals. Katherine Grainger is a case in point. Her silver medal in Sydney was a better-than-expected result, and though it would be wrong to say the experience left her expecting that gold would come easily at the next Olympics or the one after that, it is fair to say that her subsequent quest for gold was harder than she ever imagined it would be.

Ultrarealists are better able to deal with harder-than-expected experiences and rude awakenings than are other athletes. The reason is that, whereas the typical athlete doesn't want things to be harder than expected, the ultrarealist doesn't really care. Of course, every athlete gets thrown off initially by a rude awakening, but ultrarealists quickly move beyond wishing things were easier than they've turned out to be to accepting that they're not. And from there, they quickly move on to embracing the situation, going from not wishing things were easier to being glad they're harder.

Glad? Really? Let me explain. For the ultrarealist, goals exist not to be achieved but to stimulate striving and to drive progress toward the fulfillment of potential. This is why champions set goals that are hard to achieve, and why they welcome opportunities to raise their game. There is perhaps no better example of the mindset I'm talking about than Ajeé Wilson, the finest 800-meter runner the US has ever produced. Throughout her career, Ajeé has run in the shadow of Caster Semenya, a virtually unbeatable South African half-miler who has been barred more than once from competing as a woman because she has XY chromosomes and naturally high testosterone levels. There are a number of big races Ajeé would have won if Caster hadn't been in them. One of these was the 2019 Prefontaine Classic at Stanford University, where Caster, with a possible second ban looming over her, narrowly missed breaking the 800-meter world record in the process of demoting Ajeé to second place yet again. Facing a scrum of journalists immediately after the race, the American was pressed for her views on the controversy.

"Do you think it's good for the sport if Semenya is allowed to run?" asked one reporter.

"Absolutely, I think she should be allowed to run," Ajeé answered emphatically.

Another reporter then asked her a slightly different version of the same question.

"I think *everyone* should be allowed to participate," Ajeé replied, clearly losing patience.

Given the complexity of the issue, and how directly Ajeé was impacted by it, one might have expected her to support Caster's exclusion, an opinion many were voicing at the time. But Ajeé's stance was clear.

"I definitely think she should be able to do what she loves," she repeated.

"Do you think having her in the race helped push you?" one reporter asked.

"Absolutely," Ajeé replied.

Bingo! The competitor in Ajeé wanted Caster in the big races because the ultrarealist in Ajeé cared more about getting the very most out of herself than about winning. And she was right to believe that she was a better runner with Caster to vie against than without her.

Katherine Grainger exhibited the same attitude throughout her illustrious career. In the lead-up to the 2005 World Championship, news broke that Kathrin Boron, the most decorated female rower in history, had been added to a German quad that Katherine's crew had narrowly outperformed throughout that year's World Cup season. Katherine's reaction? "I knew that the stakes had been raised a little bit higher, and the odds were now stacked against us," she wrote later. "There is, however, something exciting about taking on the best in the world, those rare individuals who have broken through barriers and blazed trails."

In short: *Bring it on!*

The following year, Katherine's quad was shockingly beaten at worlds by a Russian team that was later disqualified when Olga Samulenkova failed a drug test. Katherine's reaction? "I felt we hadn't raced as well as we could have, and it was actually our own performance that let us down, not the cheating," she recalls in her memoir. "If we had raced to our full potential, then we would have won regardless of how many of the Russians had taken testosterone." While Katherine abhorred cheating, even the indisputably unfair advantage one of her competitors gained from doping was seen by her as an opportunity to stretch herself.

All athletes produce their best performances when they give their best effort, and they give their best effort when they have at least some doubt about the achievability of their goal. This was shown in a study by researchers at Michigan State University and Brock University and published in *Psychology of Sport and Exercise* in 2017. Seventy-five subjects answered questions designed to assess their self-efficacy ("an individual's belief in his or her capacity to execute behaviors necessary to produce specific performance attainments") before being asked to hold a prone plank as long as they could. Those who scored either very low or very high on the self-efficacy test failed to hold the plank as long as they expected to, whereas those in the middle matched their expectations. When the plank test was repeated, the subjects with both low and high self-efficacy scores improved, whereas those in the middle did not, indicating that only the individuals possessing realistic initial expectations for their performance had given their best effort the first time around.

During her post-race interview at Stanford in 2019, Ajeé Wilson was asked if she believed Caster Semenya was unbeatable. "I think anyone is beatable," she said, adding that, in this specific case, she might only be capable of beating her once in every "50 or 60" races. There is simply no better attitude Ajeé could have had if her true goal was to realize 100 percent of her potential.

Every athlete needs some kind of goal to perform their best, but the most successful athletes put their goals largely out of mind and devote their attention to the journey rather than to the destination. In other words, in contrast to less successful athletes, the most successful athletes are *process-focused* rather than outcome-focused. A focus on outcomes is a form of wishing, and wishing, as I have noted repeatedly, is a rejection of reality. The more energy an athlete puts into wishing for a desired outcome, the less effort they put into taking action to bring about this outcome. As R&B singer PJ put it in her song "My Best Life," "I just make it happen, I don't do a lot of wishing." It's really one or the other.

A process focus doesn't work by magic. Research indicates that it works by increasing motivation and reducing anxiety. Makes sense, right? Motivation manifests itself through engagement in a given process, and substituting wishing with doing fosters a sense of control, which is inherently anxiety-reducing. Evidence of how a process focus works beneficially in an exercise-specific context comes from a 2009 study published in the *International Journal of Sport and Exercise Psychology*. Kylie Wilson of the University of Wales and Darren Brookfield of Edge Hill University recruited 60 volunteers to participate in a six-week exercise program. Before they started, the subjects were divided into a process-goal group, an outcome-goal group, and a control group. Members of the first group worked with Brookfield to come up with appropriate process goals, an example being "Maintain your heart rate above 140 beats per minute for 30 minutes of your 40-minute session." These goals were then updated on a weekly basis through the program. Members of the second group developed and revised individual outcome goals (e.g., "Lose four kilograms in six weeks") through a similar process, and members of the control group went through the program without goals.

At the beginning and again at the end of the program, all of the subjects completed a test called the Intrinsic Motivation Inventory. On average, the process-goals group reported high levels of "initial interest and enjoyment" and "perceived choice" and even higher levels of both six weeks later, whereas the outcome-goals group experienced a steep decline in these motivational measures. Meanwhile, self-ratings of tension and stress were initially lower in the process-goals group and dropped further, a stark contrast to what was observed in the outcome-goals group. Finally, the process-goals group skipped fewer workouts than the outcome-goals group, not only during the six-week program but for the next four-and-a-half months of follow-up monitoring. Overall, Wilson and Brookfield concluded, focusing on the exercise process instead of on desired outcomes led to more enjoyment, a greater sense of control, less anxiety, *and better outcomes.*

Process goals should be integrated into your own training at every level, from individual workouts to training blocks to training cycles to multiyear development. Examples of process goals are holding back enough in the first few intervals of a high-intensity interval workout to ensure you're able to make the last interval your fastest, doing a better job of mixing up your strength exercise selection from week to week, getting in at least eight massage therapy appointments before your next big race, and increasing your peak weekly training volume by 10 percent in each of the next three training cycles. Individually, such goals will benefit you in ways similar to the ways they benefitted the subjects in the Wilson and Brookfield study, and collectively they will make you a more process-focused athlete who's better able to make the best of harder-than-expected situations.

A process focus is probably the defining feature of Katherine Grainger's athletic psychology. It came to her naturally. In 1997, when she was a rookie member of the British National Rowing Team, Katherine and three fellow greenhorns were assigned the daunting challenge of racing the current senior quad on the training course at Holme Pierrepont. If they finished within one boat length of them, they would earn the right to join the seniors in the eight that would represent Great Britain at the World Championships. If not, their elite rowing careers would likely be over almost before they'd begun. At the end of her first practice session with her new crew, Katherine spontaneously initiated a visualization exercise, guiding the others through an imagined version of the impending match race as they rowed the course together at a relaxed pace. This exercise was repeated each day thereafter until the real event took place, Katherine envisioning a different scenario each time and inviting her boatmates to join her in envisaging precisely how they would handle it individually and collectively. By the end of this process, they all felt ready for anything, and they achieved their goal. Mental rehearsals like these are an effective tool for focusing your mind on *how*—rather than *whether*—you will achieve success in your next event.

Katherine's natural process focus was reinforced in the years to come by Chris Shambrook, the staff psychologist for British Rowing. In a meeting with Chris before the 2003 World Championships in Milan, Katherine and her crewmate in the coxless pair, Cath Bishop, communicated their shared desire to avoid obsessing about the end result and concentrate on the goal of finding out how fast their boat could go. Chris readily endorsed this process-focused attitude, and offered Katherine and Cath a clever little trick to support it in the heat of competition. The rowers were instructed to picture a trampoline at the finish line, tipped onto its side so that any thought of theirs that jumped ahead to the outcome would bounce back to the present moment. They bought into it and it worked. When Katherine found her boat mired in fourth place in the early part of the race, she merely took note of the situation, attaching no emotion to it and continuing to devote her attention to executing each stroke perfectly. The outcome of this blindness to outcome was her first senior world championship title. Personally, I love the trampoline image, and I share it often with athletes I work with who struggle to maintain a process focus.

THE ENJOYMENT FACTOR

The pain of losing the final of the 2008 Olympic women's quadruple sculls followed Katherine home, a heavy piece of unwanted emotional baggage. At a homecoming event held for returning British Olympians and their families, Katherine overheard a conversation between another athlete and her mother, the athlete bubbling over with pride and joy in the silver medal she had earned. It was just the thing Katherine needed to nudge her back into a healthy perspective on her situation, yet it had no such effect, nor did any of the pep talks she received from well-meaning friends and family members. Far from abating in the weeks and months that followed her desultory return from China, Katherine's pain merely evolved, transitioning by stages from the soul-rending feeling she'd experienced at the moment of defeat into a dull, ever-present grief.

In the winter, needing both a distraction and some time alone, Katherine made a solo trip to South Africa and Namibia. It was there, in the company of primordial landscapes, exotic beasts, and her own heart, that she decided to grant her mother her wish and try for a fourth Olympics. But it could not simply be a matter of soldiering on as before, with her heart set on London gold. Rather, she wrote in *Dreams Do Come True*, "I had to be sure that, regardless of the results, I wouldn't feel it was four years wasted. There would be a lot of hard work, with no guarantee of a happy ending. It had to be about enjoying the daily challenge and the company rather than clinging on just to see if I could win gold. Without question, that goal would be the driving force, but I had to buy into the entire four-year journey and not just one day in August 2012."

Smart move. In the previous section, we saw that a process focus increases enjoyment and improves outcomes. But it's also true that increasing enjoyment enhances process focus, which in turn improves outcomes. This two-way causal connection has been abundantly demonstrated in educational research. In both children and adults, efforts to make learning tasks more enjoyable have been shown to increase engagement and attentional focus, partly through neural mechanisms such as elevated release of the neurotransmitter dopamine, which is associated with reward.

Studies in sports psychology and exercise physiology have yielded similar findings. A study conducted by scientists at the University of Worcester and published in 2020 in the *International Journal of Sports* found that runners performed better and reported higher levels of positive affect (enjoyment) in a 10K group race than in a 10K solo time trial. Because pacing strategies did not differ between the two conditions, the authors of the study were left to conclude that heightened enjoyment was the cause of the performance boost runners got in the group race.

Other research, including a 2016 case study involving West Virginia University's women's soccer team, suggests that a shift toward a process focus is indeed the mechanism that links enjoyment and better performance. WVU sports science professor Scott Barnicle divided the team into two groups—a treatment group that was subjected to an enjoyment-focused mental skills training (MST) program and a control group that was left alone—and then monitored both over the course of an entire competitive season. According to Barnicle, "The 12-week intrinsic enjoyment-focused MST program was focused on promoting and enhancing intrinsic sources of sport enjoyment" such as "competitive excitement" and "effort expenditure," and it succeeded. Between the start and end of the season, members of the treatment group registered a 4.5 percent increase in intrinsic enjoyment of the game of soccer and a more than twofold increase in performance as measured by game statistics and coach evaluations, whereas the controls showed a decline in enjoyment and a more modest increase in performance. Barnicle's star subject, "Sarah," who struggled with buy-in initially, saw a 19.3 percent increase in enjoyment coupled with a 100 percent increase in points scored between the first and second halves of the season, improvements that occurred in parallel with a 13.3 percent bump in process-focused performance.

Literally *anything* you can do to augment your enjoyment of training will facilitate a process focus and lead to better performance. If you will enjoy a given workout more in location A than in location B, you'll get more out of it in location A. If you will enjoy a workout more with training partner C than with training partner D, you'll get more out of it with training partner C. If you will enjoy a given workout more with music than without, you'll get more out of the workout with music. And so on.

Katherine Grainger's decision to toss her hat into the ring of the London Olympics was shaped by an almost hardwired understanding of the enjoyment-process-focus-performance connection that she owed to formative experiences. At the time of her birth in Glasgow, Scotland, both of Katherine's parents worked as secondary school teachers, and both loved their jobs. Then her father, Peter, took a position in national curriculum development, and although it paid better, he did not enjoy the work. Five days a week, Katherine saw her mom come home from school in a happy mood and her father return from the office looking defeated, and the contrast made an abiding impression, leaving Katherine resolved to prioritize enjoyment in her career.

So it was that, upon landing back in the UK after two weeks in Africa, Katherine informed her coach, Paul Thompson, that she wished to compete as a single sculler in the 2009 season. It seemed an odd decision to Thompson, who knew Katherine as an extrovert who relished the team aspect of rowing, but from her point of view the crucial thing was that rowing individually would be new, fresh, and different, and as such it would not saddle her with expectations based on past success. "I wanted to recapture my love and passion for the sport," she explained in her autobiography, and her gut told her this was the way to do it.

Thompson couldn't just rubber-stamp the plan, however. To earn the right to represent Great Britain in the single scull, Katherine would have to win the national team trials in February, and she did. Then she won the first world cup race of the 2009 season, and all of a sudden she was saddled with expectations that threatened to vitiate her focus on simply enjoying the process. Things came to a head in the lead-up to the World Championships in Poland, where Katherine struggled to reconcile her desire to just have fun with an inner admission that it was impossible for her to have fun unless she was performing well.

After meeting with Chris Shambrook to discuss her conundrum, the psychologist sent her a link to a clip from the television show *Friends*. It showed Lisa Kudrow's character, Phoebe, jogging in Central Park in such a comically spastic manner that her friend Rachel, played by Jennifer Aniston, refused to be seen with her. But eventually Phoebe's childlike enjoyment of running her way and her total lack of self-consciousness won Rachel over, and she came up with her own goofy gait. The clip inspired Katherine to set aside external performance standards and race her way, aiming to be the best Katherine Grainger she could be rather than the best sculler. "Remember Phoebe," she said to herself at the start line of the World Championship final on a choppy Lake Malta. She then proceeded to smile her way to a silver medal and a new British national record for 2,000 meters.

That was enough of solitary rowing for Katherine, however, and after she successfully defended her trials title in 2010, she elected to pair up with runner-up Anna Watkins in a double scull. The two women had been thrown together recently in training and discovered an instant chemistry, a complementarity the likes of which Katherine had never experienced with any other athlete in her long career on the water. With Anna she didn't have to try to enjoy herself—the fun was woven into each harmonious stroke.

Performance followed. The new British women's double sculls team won all three World Cup events of 2010 and capped the season with a dominating performance at the World Championships in New Zealand, beating their closest competitors by more than five seconds. The following year, Anna missed the first World Cup with a back injury, then came down with food poisoning at the World Championships in Slovenia. She and Katherine won anyway, keeping their undefeated streak alive, their bond further strengthened by adversity.

When the indomitable duo arrived at Dorney Lake, site of the London Games' rowing events, they remained unbeaten, having won three more World Cup events and set an unofficial 2,000-meter world record in training. While scoping out the venue, Katherine bumped into Marnie McBean, a three-time Olympic champion from Canada. In the course of catching up, Marnie brought up the concept of "the want-to sweet spot," which she had learned from sport psychologist Cal Botterill, describing it as a sort of Goldilocks zone between not caring whether you succeed or fail and feeling as though you *have to* succeed and *mustn't* fail. It was a timely last-minute reminder to Katherine to race with passion rather than fear.

During training the next day Anna spontaneously burst out laughing, and there was no need for Katherine to ask why—the boat felt *that* good. By now the outcome was a foregone conclusion. The host nation's representatives in the women's double scull won their heat in a rout and, despite an unfavorable lane placement, they led the final from start to finish, inciting pandemonium in the grandstands. It had been harder than she ever expected, but at long last Katherine Grainger had her Olympic gold.

The end.

Or not. In October 2014, Katherine ended a two-year retirement to give it one last shot. She would be 40 years old when the Rio Games rolled around. "It's going to be hard," Katherine told an Olympic Channel interviewer on her first day back in a boat. But it turned out to be even harder than that—indeed, another rude awakening.

Always well-liked by her fellow athletes, Katherine could not have antic-ipated that a clash of personalities, of all things, would be the factor that made a successful comeback not just hard but almost impossible. For the 2015 season, Katherine was paired with Vicky Thornley, a 6′4″ former model 12 years her junior. In that year's European Championships, the new part-ners scored a bronze medal that might have been gold if not for a couple of midrace mistakes that each blamed the other for, and they regressed from there, finishing out of the medals entirely in the following year's European Championships. By then they were barely on speaking terms, and the deci-sion to dissolve their partnership was the first thing they'd agreed on in some time. Only after both women failed to qualify for the eight did they agree to bury the hatchet and try to make it work, earning selection as the British representatives in the women's double sculls just two months before the Opening Ceremony in Brazil. Considered a long shot to make the final at Rodrigo de Freitas Lagoon, they not only did so but led the final until the 1,800-meter buoys, where Poland clawed past them to steal gold by less than a second. Silver again. So disappointing, right? Wrong.

"That's why you don't see tears, you don't see upset, you don't see dis-appointment," Katherine said in a post-race interview for the Olympic Channel with Vicky at her side. "Because I genuinely don't know what more we could have done. The aim for every athlete at this level is to put out your best possible performance for the day, and if it's absolutely spot on, you're better than everyone else, you come away with the gold. I think we put out our best possible performance today, and it was good enough for most of the race to be gold and in the end it was silver . . . And I'm happy with that."

7 DAYS TO SANTA ROSA

Ironman Santa Rosa is one week from today, and—not a moment too soon—I'm feeling pretty good about my running. More than that, though, I'm feeling good about the road I took to reach this point.

About four months ago, I suffered yet another setback with my groin. I didn't do anything stupid—at least not anything stupider than taking the small risk of running very slowly every other day and of very gradually increasing the distance of my longest runs as my pain allowed. But in January, when I was 55 minutes into what was supposed to be a 60-minute run, there came a point where the pain level was unacceptably high no matter how slowly I went, and I decided to stop. In the same moment, I also decided that I'd had my last setback. I simply could not afford another one, and I would make damn sure I didn't have one, even if this required that I not run another step until race day.

Aware that when ultrarealists find themselves in such situations, they improvise, or scramble, I challenged myself to do the same. Instead of stubbornly insisting on taking a familiar road from where I was to the sort of run fitness I hoped to have for Santa Rosa, I created a new road.

When I can't run, I like to walk at a steep incline on a treadmill because it closely emulates both the cardiovascular and neuromuscular demands of running, but with less impact, so the fitness earned through the activity transfers over to running fairly directly. Still, it's not running.

So, I planned to try a little *jogging* at a 15 percent incline, and if that went well, to run slightly faster at a slightly lower gradient a few days later, and so on until I was able to run normally again. With this approach, I hoped, I could continue building up my running fitness, without hindering my recovery.

Well, it worked. On Valentine's Day, I ran for an hour at 7 mph and a 4 percent incline, not pain-free but with an acceptable level of discomfort. Two days later, I ran at the same speed with no incline, and four days after that I ran outdoors for the first time since the aborted run a month earlier. But I wasn't out of the woods—far from it, in fact. Yes, I was running outside again, and I could go as long as I pleased without aggravating my groin, but I was still quite limited in terms of pace, anything faster than 8:30 per mile causing warning signals to issue from the afflicted area. So I decided to go back to the treadmill, but not exclusively, mixing long, slow outdoor runs to build the endurance I needed with faster, uphill treadmill runs to build the speed I needed to perform as I hoped to in Santa Rosa.

Each year, in late March, I run the Modesto Marathon, the biggest annual running event in my area. I had signed up for this year's event months ago, intending to complete it as a workout, cruising the distance at or near my Ironman goal pace of 7:30 per mile. Still unable to safely run at this pace on race day, I started with a cautious 8:49 mile, and then went by feel. I was around the halfway point when I realized that my improvised training strategy had paid off. I completed mile 17 in 7:55, my first sub-8:00 mile in ages. What's more, my groin said I could go faster, so I went faster, covering mile 22 in 7:29 and mile 26 in 6:51, drunk with gratitude for the hard-won return to health.

Another marathon I like to run often is Boston, and I was more or less obliged to run it this year—even though it fell just 15 days after Modesto and 26 days before my Ironman—because I had a new book to promote there. Again, though, my goal was not to go all-out but to run a controlled effort that served to build me up instead of breaking me down. More specifically, I hoped to sneak under three hours without killing myself. But the training I'd done leading into it was so unconventional that I didn't have a good sense of whether this hope was realistic. Running entirely by feel, I found a comfort zone around 6:40 per mile and stayed there the whole way, finishing in 2:54:08.

Determined to make as much additional progress with my running as I could in the little time I had, I tested my groin's ability to survive a set of mile repeats nine days after Boston. It held up, so I reprised the session a week later, pushing a little harder. Again the pain was minimal, so three days later— today—seeking one last fitness-boosting stimulus, I ran a half-marathon. The goal this time was to put in a 90 percent effort, which translated into overall victory and a finish time of 1:17:56.

I almost can't believe my running has come this far since January. It's no miracle, however. It's a testament to the power of addressing the reality of a bad situation by finding a way instead of forcing a way. In the past, like many athletes, I've failed to make the best of a bad situation by trying to make a certain plan or familiar course of action work even though on some level I knew I was bullshitting myself. Not this time.

8

COMING BACK
FROM SELF-SABOTAGE

I paint with my qualities and faults.

VINCENT VAN GOGH, AS PLAYED BY WILLEM DAFOE
IN THE FILM *AT ETERNITY'S GATE*

SOMETIMES THE HARDEST REALITY to face is the reality of oneself. Every athlete—every human being—is a messy jumble of gifts, hang-ups, strengths, and weaknesses. We are all special, and we are all imperfect, and as athletes we may find that our imperfections periodically cause us to commit acts of self-sabotage. That's a loaded word, I know, because it's often used in a blaming sort of way, but that's not how I'm using it here. For me, *self-sabotage* is simply the right word to describe bad situations that, unlike the bad breaks and rude awakenings we've discussed in the preceeding two chapters, are created by an athlete's own behavior.

Consider the example of overtraining, a common type of self-sabotage in sports. Except in cases where athletes are forced to overtrain by a poor coach, it is the overtrained athlete himself or herself who is responsible for digging the hole that must now be climbed out of. Frequently, the underlying cause of overtraining is lack of confidence, a persistent doubting of one's fitness that leads to a pattern of excessive work and insufficient rest. But lack of confidence is not something that anyone can be blamed for.

More often than not, an athlete's lack of confidence stems from past experiences they had no control over.

Coming back from self-sabotage is especially tricky because the root source is usually an ingrained element of one's personal makeup. Correcting self-sabotage is therefore different from, say, removing a tumor, where the lump inside you can be cleanly excised from your body. Removing a part of your personal makeup is not a viable way to correct self-sabotage. This is why so many men and women who are recovering from substance abuse, for example, get into endurance sports. Recognizing that they cannot entirely eradicate their addictive tendencies, they figure it's better to replace an unhealthy dependency with a healthy obsession than to try futilely to change what cannot be changed.

If you look at multiple cases where athletes have successfully overcome some of the more extreme varieties of self-sabotage, you will find they all do it in the same fundamental way. In each case, the comeback is not a mere matter of kicking a habit. Rather, it's a matter of accepting, embracing, and addressing the reality of oneself, through a process that the philosopher Friedrich Nietzsche calls *becoming who you are.*

In colloquial terms, becoming who you are means working with what you've got. By the time we reach adulthood, much of what is inside us—gifts, hang-ups, strengths, and weaknesses—may always be inside us. In the effort to overcome self-sabotage, we cannot simply get rid of all of our hang-ups and weaknesses. That would amount to becoming a different person, which is impossible. What *is* possible, however, is evolving into a better version of yourself, and herein lies the key to beating self-sabotage. Nietzsche describes this process as "giving style to one's character," likening it to the way great artists work with what's inside them to achieve true originality, if never perfection. This "great and rare art," he writes, "is exercised by those who see all the strengths and weaknesses of their own natures and then comprehend them in an artistic plan until everything appears as art and reason and even weakness delights the eye."

Even the most talented artists have flaws and limitations that no amount of training can overcome, just as even the most exceptional individuals have hang-ups and quirks that no amount of personal growth can erase. The artists we consider great are those who make their flaws and limitations somehow complement their strengths and contribute to their signature style—artists like Billie Holiday, who made her eccentric timbre and compressed vocal range essential elements of her signature world-weary, old-soul singing style. Likewise, the athletes who achieve greatness despite having self-sabotaging tendencies do so not by changing who they are but by becoming who they are. Let's examine three case studies and identify the specific lessons they teach others seeking the benefits of facing the reality of themselves.

PAUL THOMAS: DUATHLETE, JONAH COMPLEX SUFFERER

In his 1971 book *The Farther Reaches of Human Nature*, psychologist Abraham Maslow introduced the concept of the Jonah complex. Often defined as a fear of success, the biblically allusive term refers more specifically to a fear of standing out, or being perceived as arrogant or bigheaded, or accepting the burden of one's gifts, or conceding one's superiority in a particular skill or role. Most of us are susceptible to occasional Jonah moments, so to speak, but an unlucky few develop the full-blown complex, consistently standing in the way of their own success, and the one thing these modern-day Jonahs all have in common is low self-worth. Simply put, they don't feel *deserving* of success.

When I think of athletes who have been held back by low self-worth, I think of Paul Thomas. The source of Paul's Jonah complex is no mystery, sadly. One of his earliest memories is of being stuffed into the back of the family sedan with his older brother, Jimmy, and his infant sister, Mary, and driven into the desert outside Salt Lake City, where the three siblings were forced to watch their drunken father savagely beat their mother. The following year, Paul's dad was shot in the leg by police officers while resisting arrest for driving under the influence of alcohol. Instead of hanging around to face the music, he went on the lam, taking nothing with him except (unlucky for them) his wife and children, coming to rest eventually in Sacramento, where Paul would spend the balance of his childhood.

The real damage to Paul's emotional well-being was done not so much by such explosive events as by his father's daily, almost programmatic, efforts to crush his second child's self-esteem. For reasons he never understood, Paul was singled out for special maltreatment by the Thomas family patriarch, subjected to a never-ending program of criticism, bullying, and punishment. "You'll never make as much money as I do," his dad told him, not once but often, a prophesy made all the more stinging by the fact that Paul's father did not exactly rake in the dough as a sheet metal welder. No matter what Paul did, the man who should have been his loudest cheerleader saw nothing but failure and disappointment in his future.

When Paul discovered running—and almost immediately thereafter, success—as a preteen, nothing changed except the content of these paternal verbal beatdowns. "You'll be just as fat as I am when you're my age," became the new refrain after Paul's racing exploits began to receive attention. At age 10, Paul qualified for the finals of the junior Olympics. At 11, he broke the 10K national record for boys his age, and the next year he did it again, clocking 33:52 as a 12-year-old. In his first race as a freshman at Jesuit High School, Paul ran 15:08 for three miles on a challenging cross country course, finishing second to a senior. An article published in the *Sacramento Bee* soon afterward hailed Paul as the best young runner the city had ever produced, but the writer also noted that the 114-pound phenom was a tough interview, reluctant to talk about his success and embarrassed of his own precociousness. The Jonah complex had begun to set in.

Despite his fraught relationship with success, Paul's sheer talent and his love of running allowed him to achieve enough (an indoor national championship title in the mile, a California State Championship title at 3,200 meters) at Jesuit to earn a full scholarship at the University of Arkansas, which boasted the nation's strongest running program at the time. But he squandered the opportunity, gaining 13 pounds of beer weight in his first semester and going downhill from there, ultimately losing his scholarship and transferring to the University of Arizona in Tucson, where his collegiate running career ended with surgery to repair a torn iliotibial band.

Paul still loved running, but he needed a fresh start. And so, after recovering, he signed up for a duathlon, a run-bike-run race in Phoenix. Despite having done no formal bike training whatsoever, he finished seventh and came home fired up to see what he could do with a little more preparation.

A few weeks later, during a group bike ride up Mount Lemmon, Paul found himself alone off the front with a stranger. When they reached the top, his companion struck up a conversation.

"Never seen you out here," he said. "What do you do?"

"I'm a duathlete," Paul said proudly.

"Really? So am I. Name's Joel Thompson."

Paul knew the name. A local celebrity, Joel was one of the top professional duathletes of the day.

"Obviously, you can ride a bike," he said, shooting a glance back down the mountain. "But can you run?"

"Actually," Paul said, "running's my specialty."

Joel's mouth fell open. He then asked Paul, as casually as he could, if he needed a coach. Nine months later, under Joel's guidance, Paul was crowned the US national duathlon champion in Long Beach, California. Not yet 26 years old, he looked to have a bright future ahead of him in the sport—and he surely would have, if not for the Jonah thing.

The following year, perhaps predictably, Paul put more energy into hanging out at coffee shops with the cool Cat I bike racers than he put into following the workouts Joel gave him, and as a result the 1995 season was a total washout. "I've never seen anyone as talented as you," Joel said to him at one point, "but you've got to do a few things right." But the self-sabotage continued, and in 1996 Paul decided he was finished as an athlete and moved to San Diego to make another fresh start, this time as a sales rep for energy bar maker PR Nutrition.

Three years later, overworked, out of shape, and drinking too much, Paul allowed himself to be talked into participating in the Dannon Duathlon Series. He gave up alcohol and caffeine, improved his sleep habits, and started training. The new lifestyle agreed with him, and in April 1999 Paul won the Dannon series opener in Arlington, Texas. Afterward, during a quiet moment alone, he broke down unexpectedly, weeping for reasons he didn't understand. Was he happy that he won? Sorry for winning? He had no idea. In any case, he went on to sweep the entire series, including the national championship, and he didn't cry again.

"All my life I'd been telling myself, 'I'll be good next year,'" Paul told me in a 2019 phone conversation. "'Second is good enough.' But that year I told myself I wasn't going to lose anything. I wasn't going to wait for next year."

Good thing, too, because there was no next year. Recognizing that competitive success would never do for him what it seemed to do for other athletes, Paul retired from the sport again at season's end, but on his terms this time. He eventually moved back to Tucson, where his main focus today is mentoring younger athletes, especially fellow sufferers of low self-worth. Folks like Conrad, a member of the University of Arizona club triathlon team who could barely make eye contact when Paul first met him but who, over the course of four years, developed a confidence and inner strength that, even more than the training Paul gave him, powered his ascent from 330th to 79th to 33rd to 17th at the Collegiate National Triathlon Championship.

Done with running, Paul still rides a bike, competing just often enough to scratch that itch to see what he can do and, for better or worse, still winning. In 2018, at 50, he won the Arizona State Time Trial Championship, and the following year he successfully defended his title. The combined age of the second- and third-place finishers was 52.

"Maybe I could have gone to the Olympics," Paul told me in our phone interview. "But if I had a choice between doing that and then quitting and gaining 60 pounds like a lot of athletes I know or still exercising at a pretty high level in my fifties, I would choose this. All I do is ride, mostly with people who are much slower than me. I don't do it to impress anyone or prove anything. I do it because I can. It's a way to have the wind blowing in my face, just like when I was a kid, except now I'm not running from anything."

MOLLY SEIDEL: RUNNER, PAST DISORDERED EATER

Molly Seidel's obsessive-compulsive disorder has been with her almost as long as she can remember. Raised in the tiny town of Hartland, Wisconsin, she felt frequent urges to touch objects and surfaces in specific patterns, something no other kid she knew seemed to do. Her thoughts often raced in circles, searching for a sense of control they never found. Anxiety was her baseline emotion, as inescapable as gravity unless she had some kind of distraction.

When she started running competitively in the seventh grade, Molly discovered a whole new way of being that remains accessible to her to this day. "I feel most like myself when I am running," she explained on the *Running on Om* podcast in 2019. "My mind just perfectly fits into the vessel of my body. Everything makes sense."

It didn't hurt that Molly was good at running—really good. As a freshman at University Lake School, she won state titles in cross country and on the track at 1600 and 3200 meters, then repeated the feat in each of the next three years, capping her brilliant high school running career with a victory at the 2011 Foot Locker Cross Country Championship. At the time, no female Foot Locker winner had ever gone on to win the NCAA Cross Country Championship, but three years later, as a junior at Notre Dame, Molly did just that.

The achievement came at a cost, however. Burdened by intense pressure to live up to the standard she'd established for herself, Molly developed an eating disorder, not so much because she wanted to look a certain way, as is so often the case, but for the sense of control it gave her. The consequences, in any case, were all too typical. Her bones turned fragile, and she suffered a succession of stress fractures and breaks, and yet she somehow won three more NCAA titles before graduating.

Her trajectory was unsustainable, however, a collision with rock bottom inevitable. It came at the 2016 Olympic Track Trials in Eugene, Oregon, where Molly, injured again, was a spectator, not a competitor. Her friend and Notre Dame teammate Dani Aragon sat her down there and gave her the news she needed to hear.

"You're not okay," Dani said. "You look like you're dying."

Two days later, Molly checked herself into an eating disorder treatment facility back home in Wisconsin. Six months of inpatient care were followed by two years of therapy. Throughout this process, Molly never gave up on running because she knew she needed it to be happy, regardless of whether she ever won another race. But her happiness also required that she approach running in the right way. That's why, after signing a professional running contract with Saucony and moving to Boston, she established an almost-daily donut habit and took side jobs as a nanny and a barista. Although donuts are not considered the best recovery food for runners, indulging in them helps Molly maintain a more relaxed attitude toward food generally. And whereas most elite runners try to relax as much as possible when they're not training, Molly knows that she functions best and is least likely to go to dark places in her mind when she's busy. As she put it to podcaster Julia Hanlon, "You need to be mentally well in order to run your best."

In February 2020, Molly became Exhibit A in support of this claim. Having qualified for the Olympic Trials Marathon with a 1:09:35 half-marathon in Houston the previous month, she came to Atlanta with three goals: to "send it" (the credo she shares with her current coach, John Green), to gain experience in the marathon (she'd never run one), and to finish somewhere between 10th and 20th. Molly achieved two of these goals, and far exceeded the third, crossing the line in second place with a time of 2:27:31 and qualifying for the Tokyo Olympics.

LIONEL SANDERS: TRIATHLETE, RECOVERING ADDICT

There is a *thing* in Lionel Sanders's soul—some mysterious force, or drive, or energy—that he can't quite define but that nevertheless defines him. It's the thing that impels him to pursue suffering in his triathlon training with an animal ferocity that makes other athletes' talk of visiting the pain cave seem like just that: talk. Oftentimes, in the middle of a hard indoor ride, Lionel lets out a primal scream of rage, or torment, or some mix of the two. Once, in 2015, his fiancé (now wife), Erin MacDonald, grabbed her phone to video one of these episodes, instead capturing him bursting into a spontaneous fit of weeping even as he continued to pedal.

This *thing* inside him is also what caused Lionel to throw away a promising high school cross country running career in his hometown of Harrow, Ontario, by smoking pot before practice and ditching workouts as soon as he left his coach's sight. Later, at McMaster University, he gave cocaine a try. One thing led to another, and before long he was on an unspoken mission to see how high he could get. Lionel dropped out of college and took a succession of jobs to earn the money he needed to support his spiraling habit. Coke remained his drug of choice, but he also drank heavily and, in a pinch, took whatever he could get his hands on: hallucinogens, glue, even a handful of mystery pills cadged from a complete stranger on one occasion.

More self-destructive behavior followed. Lionel smashed the window of a moving car with his face during a drunken blackout in an attempt to escape the vehicle. He hassled an ex-girlfriend to the point where she shared some of his voice messages with family members with instructions to pass them along to the police in the event that "something happened" to her. On his worst night, he looped one end of a belt around his neck, affixed the other end to a ceiling beam in his garage, and climbed onto a chair, intending to hang himself.

All of this drama was punctuated by stints in detox, but in the end it wasn't these enforced resets that led to Lionel's recovery. It was the crazy, bolt-from-the-blue notion to do an Ironman that struck him one day in

2009, a week after he made an equally impulsive decision to start running again. You won't find a self-help book or a 12-step program anywhere that recommends training for and completing an Ironman as step one in the process of beating an addiction, but Lionel's instincts insisted it was the right move for him. He knew snuffing out whatever it was inside that defined him was not possible; he had to redirect it.

"I think if I devote myself to training for this race, it will change me, make me a better person, give me discipline, make me feel better about myself," Lionel explained to his mother in the process of hitting her up for money to cover the cost of registering for Ironman Louisville 2010. The training in fact did all of these things, and Lionel's success (he finished near the top of his age group in Louisville) gave him all the more reason to keep going. In 2013, after sweeping the Ontario multisport Canada triathlon series, he turned pro. The next year he won three Ironman 70.3 events and his debut pro Ironman in Florida. In 2015 he won four more Ironman 70.3s and Ironman Arizona, and the following season he set a new Ironman world record of 7:44:29 in defending his title in Tempe.

I became a Lionel Sanders fan while watching live online coverage of the 2017 Ironman World Championship. After scorching the bike course in 4:14:19—a time that would have broken the course record if Cameron Wurf hadn't just ridden 82 seconds faster—Lionel passed Cam early in the marathon to take the lead. But all was not well. By the halfway point of the run, Lionel had developed a noticeable limp. I'd seen enough races to know that it was only a matter of time before he dropped out—that no amount of adrenaline or desire could enable him to grind out 13 more miles with an injury that was already bad enough to make his stride painful just to watch.

But I was wrong. Lionel not only kept going but kept going quickly, lurching his way through 6:40 miles, his form now bordering on grotesque. At one point my wife came into my office to ask if everything was okay. I'd been shouting at my computer screen, begging Lionel to stop. I thought he was destroying himself.

By the time Patrick Lange passed Lionel at 23 miles, I had a lump in my throat. Although I couldn't have articulated what I was feeling at the time, in retrospect I think I understood that, whatever it was that allowed Lionel to do what he was doing, it was both a gift and a curse. I recognized that he was, in a sense, sacrificing himself for us, his fellow athletes, going farther than any of us ever could to show us we can all go a little farther than we think.

BECOMING WHO YOU ARE

Embedded in these case studies are concrete lessons on how any athlete can overcome (or mitigate) self-sabotage by accepting, embracing, and addressing the reality of himself or herself. Five lessons in particular are worth highlighting.

Define Your Best Self

Step one in facing the reality of yourself is understanding yourself. After all, you can't work with what you've got until you know what you've got to work with. The ultimate goal is to become your best self, and to do this, you must first identify the parts of you that you most want to nurture.

The part of himself that Paul Thomas most wants to nurture is his empathy, a quality he developed initially as a survival skill at home, where he was constantly "taking temperature readings, trying to keep the peace," as he put it to me. Paul's aversion to the spotlight may have hindered him as an athlete, but the flipside of this aversion—his gift for making others feel seen—has arguably made him a better mentor than he ever was a racer.

For Molly Seidel, the mission is essentially to become more and more the person she is when she runs. When she competes, Molly almost always does so without a plan. "You just kind of let the experience take you," she said to one interviewer. Letting the experience take her is exactly what Molly's OCD *won't* let her do oftentimes in everyday life. But over the years she's gotten better at going with the flow. In 2018, Molly was forced to stop running for six months after receiving a bone graft on a hip that hadn't fully healed from a prior stress fracture. Those six months were no picnic, but instead of moping about the situation, she found other activities to immerse herself in, including writing, adventure walking, and rock climbing.

Lionel Sanders may not have a name for the fire in his soul that compels him to do everything all the way, but he has learned that if he can't contain it, he can at least steer it in a better direction. "I sort of figured out how to use my personality in a healthy, more positive way," Lionel said in a 2015 *Vancouver Sun* interview. "In the past, I used the exact same characteristics in negative, self-destructive ways." This is what it means to work with what you've got.

Be an Open Book

A striking commonality among these three overcomers of self-sabotage is how open they are about their pasts, their personal challenges, and their mistakes. Paul Thomas is disarmingly frank about his self-sabotage and his struggles with self-worth. "I really don't know how to be good," he said to me, uttering these words with a mixture of bemusement and amusement, as though he were describing a close friend whose eccentricities were both endearing and often exasperating to him.

Similarly, Molly Seidel has discussed her mental health diagnosis and her eating disorder in numerous interviews, even applying words like "crazy" and "psychotic" (while acknowledging their political incorrectness) to her inner antics. And while some prominent individuals only go public with such stuff when they consider it all behind them, or pretend it's all behind them when it's really not, Molly readily admits that her challenges remain with her every day, some days more than others.

It's the same with Lionel Sanders. When he first traded cocaine for endorphins, he felt ashamed of who he'd been and what he'd done, using swimming, cycling, and running as vehicles for fleeing his past. But no longer. Prior to a 2020 redesign, if you were to have stumbled upon Lionel's personal website knowing nothing about him, the first thing you would have learned was that he's a former drug addict. Triathlon wasn't even mentioned on the homepage.

In being so open, these athletes are not glorifying their struggles and mistakes; rather, they're demonstrating self-acceptance. To become the person you want to be, you must fully acknowledge the person you are. Nurturing the parts of you that you're most glad for is important, but no less important is managing the parts you might wish didn't exist at all. That's the other side of working with what you've got. Paul would never have chosen to "not know how to be good," nor would Molly have chosen her OCD, nor Lionel his susceptibility to addiction, but each recognizes the reality of these parts of their self and makes the best of them, like chefs on a competitive cooking show making the best of an ingredient they're required to use in a dish it doesn't really belong in.

The true test of self-acceptance is transparency. If there's a part of you that you try to hide from others, you best believe you're also hiding it from yourself. I'm not saying you have to go and bare your soul on Facebook, but you certainly should share your whole self with the people closest to you. It can be a scary step to contemplate, but the moment you take it, fear gives way to relief and liberation. Let your freak flag fly, as they say.

Surround Yourself with People Who Appreciate You

Relationships are an underappreciated source of self-knowledge. In fact, it is mainly through our social interactions that we learn who we are. This dependency of self-knowledge on relationships is something you can use to your advantage in the effort to get past self-sabotage and become who you are. All of us have people in our lives, or are capable of finding people, who "get" us, appreciating not merely what we do for them but the qualities that make us unique. By surrounding yourself with such people, you can accelerate the process of discovering and accepting yourself.

Paul Thomas probably would not have come as far as he has if not for his wife, Noreen. And it's no accident that the person he chose as his life partner is the dispositional opposite of his father, who used to make Paul feel guilty about enjoying himself, to the point where he'd often hurry home from bike rides and runs to be sure he was present—and not enjoying himself—when his father returned. To this day, a needle of guilt sometimes pricks the balloon of Paul's enjoyment when he's pedaling up Mt. Lemmon or through Madera Canyon, and he feels compelled to hurry home to Noreen. Except Noreen *wants* him to enjoy himself and encourages him to exercise to his heart's content because it's who he is.

Molly Seidel has always instinctively surrounded herself with people who appreciate her. The main reason she chose Notre Dame over Stanford, which had a far stronger running program, was that she liked the women on the team, their chemistry and cohesiveness. And when her mental health went south a couple of years after she arrived on campus, the support of her teammates was a huge factor in seeing her though the storm. Another was her coach, Matt Sparks, who came to Notre Dame just before the start of Molly's third year and helped her more than he may ever fully understand simply by showing he cared about her as a person and not just as a runner. For this reason, she still consults Matt as an advisor, and would be unwilling to work with any coach who had a problem with that.

There are better places on earth than Windsor, Ontario, to be a professional triathlete, but Lionel Sanders continues to make his home there in part because it's close to his parents, who "get" him better than any other people on earth. "He was always a free bird," his dad said in a 2015 interview for *USA Today* in attempting to explain what led to his son's downward spiral several years earlier. The understanding and acceptance in these words are deeply moving. Lionel is lucky to have the parents he does, and he knows it.

Take Responsibility

As we've seen, accepting a given reality does not guarantee that you will then embrace it, nor does embracing it guarantee that you will address it to the very best of your ability. In the process of facing the reality of oneself, a common barrier to taking the next steps of embracing and addressing that reality is failure to take responsibility for one's self-sabotage. To be clear, this is not about blaming yourself; it's about not blaming other people or things and recognizing that whoever or whatever it was that put you in your situation, it's up to you to get yourself out of it.

A certain degree of character is required to rise above the temptation to blame, and Paul Thomas, Molly Seidel, and Lionel Sanders all have it. As monstrously as Paul was treated by his father, he doesn't make a big deal of it. Indeed, it wasn't until well into part two of my three-part interview with him that he brought up the physical abuse that he was forced to witness, not because he was hiding it but rather, I think, because treating it as a more central element in his story would be an impediment to moving forward.

Whenever Paul talks to John McDonnell, his former coach at Arkansas, he apologizes for wasting the scholarship he was given. That's taking responsibility. And so, too, is seeking professional counseling, which Paul did shortly after he moved back to Tucson. The particular counselor Paul saw diagnosed him with PTSD. He didn't mention *this* until part three of our interview. Far from being ashamed of the condition, Paul just doesn't want the label to strip him of agency, sending him down the dead-end path of telling himself or others, "I can't help what I do because of this thing I've got."

In interviews, Molly almost goes out of her way to describe how loving and supportive her parents have always been, emphasizing in particular the fact that, while she was growing up, her mom couldn't have cared less whether Molly ran or didn't run, and if she ran, whether she ran well or poorly, as long as she was happy. Molly wants to make it clear to others that the insatiable craving for control she often feels was not imposed on her from the outside.

Molly's willingness to take responsibility is also revealed in a crucial decision she made at the end of her collegiate running career. Having won four NCAA titles in the space of a year, she received lucrative contract offers from a number of major running shoe brands, but she turned them all down so she could focus on regaining her physical and mental health. A year later, when she finally felt ready to turn pro, only one of those companies—Saucony—was willing to take a chance on her, and their offer was a fraction of what it had been originally. It's safe to say a lot of athletes in Molly's place would have gone for the bigger, earlier payday, not just for the money itself but for the chance it afforded them to defer the hard work of healing. Obviously, few athletes will ever actually have to make such a choice, but every athlete seeking to overcome self-sabotage will encounter opportunities to avoid taking responsibility, and Molly's example is a good one to follow.

Lionel, too, takes pains to underscore the fact that he was a reasonably happy and well-adjusted person when he started down the path of substance abuse. Later, when he was in the deepest throes of his addiction, his mother begged him to forgive her for whatever she had done to make him go down this path. It would have been so easy for Lionel to reinforce her self-blaming, but he did not. And when he found himself on that chair in his garage with a belt around his neck, the thing that ultimately moved him to step down unharmed was the thought of his bereft mother going through the rest of her life believing it was all her fault, when he knew it wasn't. *That's* taking responsibility.

Help Others

The people who become most fully themselves are those who use their experiences to help others. Accepting, embracing, and addressing the reality of yourself is great, and defeating self-sabotage in the process is better still, but best of all is getting to the point where you feel you have something to offer others, something that is shaped by not only your strengths and gifts but also by your imperfections and struggles. As Toni Morrison said, "The purpose of freedom is to free someone else," and it's the same with becoming who you are. And you don't have to feel that you've completed your own journey to start helping others. Starting now will only push you further in the direction of becoming who you are—indeed, that's half the point.

This notion is beautifully immanent in how Paul Thomas expresses the work he does today with others: "I'm trying to fix myself by trying to fix other people." Paul has a nose for sniffing out individuals who could use some building up, and nothing bolsters his own self-worth like bolstering someone else's. A few months before we connected by phone, he had an encounter with a man who appeared to be living on the streets. Paul had just finished a bike ride when the man approached him and asked if the CO_2 cartridge Paul was holding was "for smoking weed." Rather than extricate himself from the situation as quickly as possible, Paul patiently explained that the cartridge was in fact for inflating bicycle tires, and a lengthy conversation ensued, in the course of which Paul discovered that the man had been a top high school runner in California at the same time Paul himself had, and that they'd actually known each other a bit back then. Paul walked away feeling confident his old racing rival had benefitted in some small way from having been treated as an equal, and the moment was healing for Paul as well.

Molly Seidel volunteers for Girls Gotta Run, an organization that uses running to help girls in Ethiopia develop "personal agency, community, and membership." She makes regular visits to Bekoji, an Ethiopian town where she's forged a special bond with one girl in particular, who dreams of becoming a professional runner too and who, thanks to Molly, may have a little more faith than she did previously that a girl need not necessarily have the perfect start in life to fulfill such a dream.

Finally, Lionel Sanders helps others by sharing his ongoing journey with the broader triathlon community. He has amassed a large and devoted following by allowing other athletes to witness his ups and downs—and there have been plenty of downs, nearly all of them associated with pushing the limits (midrace blowups, injuries, a period of under-eating, bouts of overtraining)—almost in real time. In a 2017 online poll, Lionel was rated the most popular male triathlete by a sizeable margin. And while, yes, popularity is good for Lionel's career, that's really not what motivates him. In 2015, he told a writer for *The Globe and Mail*, in reference to his dark period, "My 100 percent motivation is to inspire people and give them hope that they don't have to live like that." That all of us, in other words, have the power to transcend self-sabotage.

RACE DAY

Somewhere around Vallejo, a mantra for today's race popped into my head: *Don't panic.* This was two days ago, during the three-hour drive from Oakdale to Santa Rosa. I like to choose a mantra for each race, but on the eve of the eve of one of the biggest races I've ever done, I had nothing. Until I did.

It felt right immediately. In my one previous Ironman 17 years ago, a number of things occurred—a calf muscle cramp in the swim, a drafting penalty on the bike, a doomed feeling in the early steps of the run—that caused me to freak out a little, if not quite panic. The first such moment occurred before the race even started, when my brother Sean asked me how I was feeling as he helped me with the zipper of my wetsuit and I answered, "I'm scared shitless."

Knowing and accepting that a few things were bound to go wrong in my second Ironman as well, I felt confident that the two words my muse had given me to carry through the experience would come in handy when temptations to panic presented themselves. More than that, though, the mantra seemed to encapsulate the whole ultrarealist perspective I've worked to sustain throughout this journey. It constituted my entire mental performance plan for the race.

Sure enough, I had just started the second lap of the two-lap swim in Lake Sonoma when the self-admonishment got its first use. It was déjà vu all over again, only this time both calves cramped simultaneously, forcing me to stop kicking and let my legs drag uselessly behind me. My first thought, admittedly, was, *Oh, no!*, but my very next thought was, *Don't panic.* And I didn't—but I also didn't kick again for the remainder of the swim, and the result was a second-loop split that was 2:14 slower than the first and a disappointing overall swim time of 1:05:51. Even so, I told myself in a conscious effort to reframe the situation as I made the long run to transition, I'd beaten my previous Ironman swim time and was on track for my C goal, at least.

The next temptation to freak out came soon thereafter, in the transition tent, as I struggled to pull tight arm sleeves over wet skin, a process that was as about as slow and tedious as peeling an orange with one hand. I considered abandoning the sleeves, but the inner voice I trusted most said I couldn't risk it, reminding me of the close brush with hypothermia I'd had during a training ride in conditions similar to today's. An ultrarealist would stay rational and stick to the plan, I decided, so that's what I did, a decision that inflated my transition time from a predicted 4 minutes and change to more than 7 minutes.

Less than an hour into the ride, I was overheating, desperate to get the damn sleeves off. The best I could do without stopping was to scrunch them down around my wrists, a half-assed solution that created palpable wind drag. Not long afterward, I reached into the rear pocket of my racing suit for an energy gel and discovered that my entire stash—all six packets—was gone. When or how they'd fallen out I had no clue, nor did it matter at this point. I just needed to not panic and make up the lost calories as best I could, which I did by gobbling the energy bar slices I'd stuffed in the top tube compartment of my bike and grabbing Gatorade Endurance instead of water at aid stations.

Despite everything, at 60 miles I was still on pace to complete the bike leg under my goal time of 5:10 when a race marshal pulled up alongside me on a motorcycle. I knew even before he flashed the blue card that I was on my way to the penalty tent, and I knew, too, where my violation had occurred—on a steep hill a couple of miles back, where I got stuck behind a rider who'd given everything he had to overtake me and then immediately bogged down right in front of me. "Not again!" I grumbled, dropping my head in dismay. When I was busted for drafting at Ironman Wisconsin it was in almost identical circumstances, but at least on that occasion I was able to serve the penalty immediately, and it was only 3 minutes, whereas under the current rules I would have to continue riding for more than 30 miles to reach the next penalty tent, where I would spend 5 minutes.

By the time I lifted my head, though, I'd already shaken off the blow. Eleven months of self-schooling in ultrarealism caused me almost automatically to look for the positive side of the setback, and I found one in noticing that a certain pressure had been lifted. My chances of qualifying for Kona were now very slim, but with nothing left to lose I could race a little more freely, and I consciously chose to ride and run the rest of the way with this mindset.

The toughest climb on the bike course came on Chalk Hill Road, a 1-mile, 385-foot quad-killer with an average gradient of 7.5 percent. Climbing is my strength, though, and I got up and over it without difficulty—the first time. But there were two laps, and when I hit the same climb a second time I was a lesser athlete, forced to pedal out of the saddle in my lowest gear at maximum effort just to keep from tipping over, moving so slowly that I was grateful my bike computer had frozen earlier, sparing me from knowing just how slowly. I'd hit the wall in enough races to know I might be doing just that now, but I'd also come through enough bad patches in races to know there was a good chance I'd be fine once I got over the top. Rather than worry about the first possibility, I chose to assume the second until proven wrong. Lo and behold, I was fine once I got over the top.

In 2002, while serving my penalty, I argued with the referee who had flagged me for drafting until she threatened to disqualify me if I didn't shut up. This time I cracked jokes with the two officials stationed at the penalty tent ("Dang, these are longer than church minutes!"), not only because I didn't want to be disqualified but also because I knew they had an unpleasant job (thanks to athletes like the one I was 17 years ago), and I wanted to be a bright spot in what was surely otherwise a largely trying day for them. And also because I knew I would feel better and probably even finish the ride stronger if I kept my sense of humor. Before my five minutes were up, I peed myself, unaware that doing so was a violation of the rules punishable with a DQ. I got off with a warning, however, and I can't help but think the officials' leniency was a karmic reward for my having treated them like human beings.

Less than two miles into the marathon, my feet began to hurt. A lot. I was wearing a pair of Nike Vaporfly 4%s that I had tested in a couple of workouts and used in the half-marathon I did a week ago, with no issues. Random pains sometimes happen, though, and when they do, they're often transient, so I tried to put my feet out of mind and hope the pain went away without counting on it. Alas, 3 miles farther on the pain remained distractingly intense— perhaps a 5 out of 10. Accepting that I'd probably be dealing with it the rest of the way, I told myself that it was only pain, not an injury, and whereas an injury could stop me, mere pain could not.

Remembering that no bad situation is ever entirely bad, I looked for the good in my current situation, finding plenty. I felt fit, light, and fully capable of maintaining my goal pace to the finish line as long as I stayed on top of my fueling. The weather was close to ideal (dry and warm, not hot), the course (a tree-shaded bike path) pleasant, and the energy of the people (my fellow racers, their cheering squads, the hordes of smiling volunteers) positive.

Riding a sudden wave of gratitude, I thanked every volunteer who handed me a cup and said a word or two of encouragement to every athlete I passed, including the lead woman, whom I overtook around mile 20.

The pain in my feet never abated, but by the end I wasn't even aware of it. I crossed the finish line 50th overall with a time of 9:48:06. Within minutes I learned from my brother Sean that six other men in my age group had finished ahead of me, claiming all of the Kona slots, but the news did little to dampen my euphoria. It wasn't so much my performance that pleased me as the nearly total control I'd had over my thoughts and emotions throughout the race. Beyond helping me perform well, this chosen mental state had made a challenging and potentially stressful experience deeply enjoyable and satisfying. I had trained my mind to function in a particular way today and it worked, and I can't tell you how good that feels.

9

WHEN COMEBACKS FAIL

I can bear any pain as long as it has meaning.

HARUKI MURAKAMI

SAUL RAISIN KNOWS a thing or two about turning a negative into a positive. At age 12 he developed kyphosis, a congenital curvature of the spine that threatened to spoil the hyperkinetic lifestyle he led in Dalton, Georgia, where his days were packed from sunup to sundown with baseball, football, swimming, skateboarding, karate, and bike riding. Over the next four years, the condition steadily worsened, lessening Saul's aptitude for the many sports he enjoyed—with one notable exception.

The further his spinal cord bent, the more comfortable Saul became on the seat of a bicycle. It was as if the condition were remolding his body for the specific purpose of complementing the machine's geometry. At the same time, his chest cavity expanded, allowing his heart and lungs to grow to almost superhuman proportions. Saul finished dead last in his first mountain bike race a year after his diagnosis, but he kept pedaling, and by the time he switched over to the roads three years later, he was winning.

In August 2001, having been picked up by the Saturn Development Team, Saul finished third in the Junior National Championships Road Race, earning the opportunity to represent the US at the World Championships in Lisbon. The following summer, he was back in Europe as a member of the Ofoto squad, rising steadily toward the top of the results column in U23 races. It seemed only a matter of time before the big teams came calling, and after a heroic performance at a world cup race in 2003, where Saul singlehandedly dragged fellow American Pat McCarty to victory and then hung on to take third place himself, they did.

By his 21st birthday Saul was living the dream, a full-time professional bike racer who called Monaco home and trained and raced alongside the likes of Tour de France stage winner Thor Hushovd in the green-and-white kit of team Crédit Agricole. Team manager Roger Legeay had high hopes for the young climbing specialist, who in early testing sustained a power output of 550 watts for six minutes on the slopes of the infamous Col de la Madone, his blood lactate level never exceeding the threshold value of 4 mmol/L—numbers that not even team leader Christophe Moreau, a top-10 finisher in the Tour de France, could match. Over the next two and a half years, Saul turned promise into performance, finishing ninth overall at the Tour of Germany in 2005 and kicking off the following season with a stage win at the Tour de Langkawi.

In April, Saul returned to France with the team for Circuit de la Sarthe, a four-day stage race. Stage 1 was a 150-mile trek over rolling terrain from Mouilleron-le-Captif to Saint-Mars-la-Jaille. With just over a mile to go, on a gravel-strewn stretch of road, the action heated up as riders for several teams jockeyed to position their sprinters for the final push to the line. Amid the chaos, Saul's front wheel clipped the back wheel of the rider in front of him. Or maybe his back wheel was clipped by the front wheel of the rider behind him. Or maybe something else entirely happened. Saul doesn't remember. In fact, he doesn't remember most of the three months preceding that fateful moment, or much of the several weeks that followed.

His next clear memory is of an event that occurred more than a month later, on another continent. Saul was in his room at the Shepherd Center, a critical care facility in Atlanta, and he had just been given permission by his caregivers to check his email for the first time in forever. When he logged on, he was dumbstruck to discover more than 1,200 unread messages awaiting him, a number of them from cycling superstars including Lance Armstrong and George Hincapie. They all said pretty much the same thing—some version of, "Saul, I just want you to know that I'm praying for you, and I'm here for you." Saul's puppy-dog personality—good-natured, fun-loving, affectionate, loyal—had made him well-loved on the pro cycling tour, inspiring teammates to refer to him punningly as "notre raisin préféré" (our favorite grape). But this outpouring of goodwill went beyond anything he'd experienced. *What the hell is going on?* he wondered.

Saul turned to Google, typing his name into the search box and pressing enter. More than half a million links came up. He clicked on a CNN article headlined "Raisin in a Coma after Race Crash." The story stated that 23-year-old professional cyclist Saul Raisin had crashed while riding his bike at close to 40 mph during stage 1 of the Circuit de la Sarthe in western France. He'd suffered a broken collarbone, two broken ribs, severe contusions to his dominant left hand, and sundry abrasions in a headfirst impact with the road that simultaneously knocked him out cold and caused a violent seizure. Saul had been rushed to the nearest hospital, where rapid brain swelling sent him into a deep coma. His parents were summoned. On arriving at the hospital in Angers the next day, Jim and Yvonne Raisin were told by doctors to expect their son's death at any moment.

Reading of these long-past events, Saul was in a pretty good position to know he had not died after all. He also understood now why he couldn't move the left side of his body and why he was confined to a wheelchair. Until then it had all seemed like a bad dream: Waking up in a strange place to see Crédit Agricole team doctor Joel Ménard's worried face looming over him. Discovering that he was tethered to the bed. Being asked by a therapist to draw a stick person and proceeding to draw only the right half of a stick person. Now Saul understood that these things were not elements of a bad dream but effects of a traumatic brain injury, and he wept at the knowledge.

Saul had overcome daunting odds already to get to this point. Told that he might never walk again, Saul stood up under his own power two weeks after emerging from the coma. Just how much further he could go remained to be seen, but Saul had three things working in his favor: a heart that was nearly twice the size of a normal man's, an unwavering optimism that was nominalized in another of his many nicknames, American Dreamer, and the same fierce determination to race bikes that had prompted Saul, at 17, to fight back when USA Cycling bureaucrats attempted to block him from competing on account of his kyphosis, obtaining a note from the Raisin family physician that turned the tables.

Just 41 days after the ride that almost killed him, Saul rode again—20 minutes on a therapy bike at the Shepherd Center. He was soon riding daily, busting his ass to get his left leg to catch up to his right, loving every second of it. Indeed, being back on the bike gave Saul's overall recovery such a lift that he was released from inpatient care less than two weeks later and allowed to return with his parents to his childhood home in Dalton, where he wasted no time in beginning to train on a regular road bike propped up on a wind trainer.

By the time the Tour de France started in early July, Saul was putting in three hours a day on the trainer, swimming twice a week, and lifting weights. Before the month was out, he was able to ride on rollers, an indoor cycling set-up that requires full balance. Unsupervised outdoor riding was still forbidden, but one day, while Jim and Yvonne were out running errands, Saul snuck into the garage and rode his father's bike in small circles—his first *real* bicycling since the accident. Within another three weeks, he had official clearance from his neurologist to return to full training. Over the next several months, Saul continued to pursue his comeback with fanatical zeal, completing an eight-hour, 120-mile solo ride that included 20,000 feet of climbing—as big a ride as he'd ever done before the accident—during the week of Thanksgiving.

In January, Crédit Agricole kicked off the 2007 season with a training camp in Nice. Saul was not only present for it but even set the pace in some of the hillier rides. "It is more than a dream being here," he wrote on his blog. "It is proof that dreams come true."

He was right about that. But it's also true that dreams die sometimes. Despite his improbable progress, Saul was held out of the entire 2007 racing season on account of concerns among the team's medical staff about lingering cognitive impairments (erratic judgment, slow reaction time) and about the unknown risks of another bump on the noggin. Saul did compete in that year's USA National Time Trial Championships as an independent rider, but he finished well back, still unable to get full power out of his recalcitrant left leg.

In November, Saul returned to France to train with the team and undergo physiological and neuropsychological testing. When he came home, he was surprised to find his parents waiting for him at the airport. It wasn't a pleasant surprise. Fighting back tears, Saul's mother informed him that Roger Legeay had called the day before with the information that team doctors had judged it too chancy to allow Saul to race for Crédit Agricole. Ever.

Saul shared the news in a November 27 blog post, writing, "It is hard to take in the fact that . . . the last 13 years of hard training are now over. I always say that if you do your best in anything, be happy and content knowing you did your best. I will always stand by this motto. I did my best and gave my all to get back to the sport of professional cycling and am content with the fact I did my best and I will never ask, what if? Now it is time to move [on] and start new a new life. I am no longer Saul Raisin, cyclist . . . I am now Saul Raisin, brain injury survivor. Job hunting is not going to be fun. Any ideas? Up for hire."

Thankfully, Saul had a few things to fall back on in this time of uncertainty. One was *Tour de Life*, a newly released memoir that chronicled Saul's comeback. But his forced retirement from pro cycling had a chilling effect on the book's marketing and publicity. The popular TV show *Inside Edition* cancelled a segment on Saul that undoubtedly would have moved hundreds if not thousands of copies and led to other media opportunities.

That was a tough blow, but at least Saul still had his fiancé, Aleeza Zabriskie, who happened to be the younger sister of reigning national time trial champion David Zabriskie. The two had met at LAX in April 2007, on Saul's way home from the Tour of California, where he hosted the inaugural Raisin Hope Charity Ride, a fundraiser for a foundation he created to help brain injury survivors. A whirlwind romance ensued, and by June, Saul—a far more impulsive person since the accident—had popped the question and relocated to Aleeza's hometown of Salt Lake City. But the young lovebirds barely knew each other, and the better acquainted they became, the worse they got along. Married on December 1, they split up a few months later, forcing Saul, now 25 years old, to move back in with his parents.

Saul's foundation offered another way forward. It got off to a strong start, raising 30 grand at that first charity ride in California and tens of thousands more through subsequent rides and auctions. But it never reached a point where its namesake could draw a livable salary from directing the operation, and as the hoopla surrounding Saul's accident and recovery faded, his search for something to do with the rest of his life continued.

Despondent, Saul began to regress. His limp returned, and his short-term memory lost sharpness. Never one to give up easily, though, Saul eventually figured out a way to make the best of the situation he'd landed in: He would become a triathlete.

It made perfect sense. In high school, Saul had competed on the swim team, performing well enough to attend some national meets. In the summer between his junior and senior years, he won a local sprint triathlon. And although he was no longer racing bikes professionally, he remained an exceptionally strong cyclist, and there were no team doctors in triathlon with the authority to sideline him as a liability risk.

I interviewed Saul for *Triathlete* in October 2008. By that time he had only done one event as an adult, a low-key Olympic-distance race, but he had big ambitions and excellent support. Sponsored by running shoe brand Avia and coached by the same person who coached Bjorn Andersson of Sweden, who was currently the sport's most formidable cyclist, Saul planned to participate in several Ironman 70.3 events in 2009 and then cap the year by racing the Ironman World Championship, the sport's biggest showcase. He told me that his goal was to make people say, "Wow!"

Saul made his Ironman 70.3 debut in 2009 in New Orleans, finishing 80 minutes behind the winner in 271st place. Considering that only two years before, Saul had been in a coma he was not expected to come out of, this was truly a "wow" achievement. But it wasn't the sort of performance that would earn Saul a spot in Kona, and his subsequent results weren't much better.

I lost track of Saul soon after my profile on him was published, and I was more than a little surprised when, four years later, I learned from an interview he did for a Spanish cycling website that not much had changed. His dream of competing in the Ironman World Championship persisted even as he continued to mourn the death of his prior dream.

"It was very hard for me, and it is still hard," he said of his dismissal from Crédit Agricole. "It has been almost seven years, and I still look for work and am trying to put my life together."

It was a rather disheartening interview, all in all. This wasn't how the story was supposed to end.

SUCCESS BIAS

The term *success bias* refers to a logical error whereby success stories are taken to represent the norm rather than the exceptions to the norm they truly are. A good example of success bias is the myth of upward mobility in the United States, where inspiring "rags to riches" stories are taken as proof that anyone can climb the ladder of success, when in fact America ranks poorly in upward mobility compared to peer nations.

Another example of success bias, which hits closer to home for endurance athletes, relates to diet. Social media is rife with testimonials about intermittent fasting, the ketogenic diet, and various other diets, posted by new converts who credit the restrictions they now live by for weight loss and other health and fitness benefits, including improved endurance performance. These testimonials persuade others to adopt the same restrictions in expectation of experiencing the same results, but what they don't know is that for every social media influencer who finds success on a particular diet, there are many more who discover it to be unsustainable and quit, but who keep quiet about their experience, often out of embarrassment. As a sports nutritionist, I hear from a lot of these folks afterward, when they're ready to try a more moderate way to pursue better health and fitness through diet.

This very book is also an example of success bias. The preceding chapters highlighted examples of athletes who, by virtue of their ability and willingness to face reality, were able to pull off remarkable comebacks. I shared these stories with the intention of showing ultrarealism in practice, but in the process I may have created the impression that ultrarealism always succeeds. That isn't true. Saul Raisin is one example of an athlete who, despite having no lack of mental fortitude, fell short in his effort to achieve a great comeback. And there are many others.

During the swim leg of the 1999 Ironman World Championship, Greg Welch, who'd won the race five years earlier, felt his heart rate accelerate suddenly to a terrifying 320 beats per minute. In third place at the time, he stopped swimming and floated on his back until his ticker calmed down, then resumed swimming, only to suffer a second episode.

After completing the swim, Greg briefly contemplated dropping out of the race, but he wasn't nicknamed Plucky for nothing, so he climbed on his bike and pedaled off—and was struck yet again. In this fashion, Greg completed the entire race, finishing 11th despite suffering more than two dozen episodes of what would soon be diagnosed as ventricular tachycardia. Four heart surgeries followed. Eventually Greg was cleared for light exercise, but light exercise is not what a professional triathlete does. That's as far as his comeback got.

If the bad break that Greg Welch couldn't come back from was akin to a terrifying bomb blast, Kara Goucher's was more of an agonizing slow burn, only it was not a bad break at all, but rather a choice she'll never regret. When an elite athlete at the top of her game becomes pregnant, she's rolling the dice career-wise. Whereas many athletes are able to return to their former heights after becoming mothers, some do not. It may have nothing to do with the pregnancy per se; so many things have to line up just right for an athlete who's in the zone to stay in the zone that any significant interruption to the flow of training and competition may be impossible to fully recover from.

Kara was most certainly at the top of her game when she became pregnant by her husband, Adam Goucher, also a professional runner. She had just come off a third-place finish at the 2009 Boston Marathon, which was preceded by a third-place marathon debut in New York City, which in turn followed a silver-medal performance in the World Championships 10,000 meters. Things were going so well, in fact, that Kara kept putting off getting pregnant until, at 31, she decided waiting any longer might make it difficult for her to resume her career at the same level afterward.

I visited Kara in Portland, Oregon, early in her post-childbirth comeback to profile her for *Competitor* and found her in a state of high anxiety, comparing herself almost obsessively to the prepregnancy Kara, haunted by doubts about her ability to achieve her remaining career bucket-list goals of winning Boston and breaking the American record in the marathon. "I had a huge breakthrough last week," she said to me at one point. "I had my best speed workout, my best tempo run, and my best long run [since the start of my comeback]. I needed that."

What made Kara's comeback attempt so agonizing for her was how close she got to matching her former standards. In an odd way, the whole second act of her professional running career would have tormented her far less had it been a total flop—if the runner she used to be had been completely out of sight instead of right there in front of her, just out of reach.

Kara set a marathon PB of 2:24:52 in Boston in 2011, but it was a fast year, and she finished fifth. She won the following year's US Half Marathon Championship, but her time was nearly three minutes slower than she'd run in beating the legendary Paula Radcliffe at the Great North run three years earlier.

In search of the old magic, Kara changed coaches, then moved to Boulder, Colorado, and changed coaches again, and got a new shoe sponsor. She did everything right—ran hard but not too hard, hit the gym, ate clean, got massages, napped, saw a sports psychologist—but although some training blocks were better than others, she found that she no longer enjoyed running. "I wasn't running because I wanted to run," she told *Women's Running* in 2019, after switching from professional road and track racing to recreational trail running. "I was running because I wanted this goal that would bring closure to my career." It never came.

Matt Dixon's undoing was overtraining. He developed the habit as a youth swimmer in his native England, and while his hard work in the pool brought him a certain measure of success (a scholarship at the University of Cincinnati, British Olympic Swimming Trials appearances in 1992 and 1996), "I never raced as well as I trained," he said in a 2010 interview for slowtwitch.com. Burned out on the sport by age 22, Matt transitioned into triathlon, where the same pattern was repeated. Immediate success motivated him to turn professional in just his second season, and the pressure of elite competition motivated him to train ever harder.

Matt's victory in the 2004 Half Vineman, a premier event whose past and future winners included the likes of legends Chris Legh and Simon Lessing, is a measure of what might have been for him. But instead of going on to win more and bigger races, he slowly unraveled, developing chronic fatigue and hormonal disruptions so severe that he was forced to stop exercising entirely for several months. Even so, it wasn't the end of the world. He got his health back, he was still young, and he knew that talent doesn't just go away. On paper, Matt had every reason to attempt a comeback. But the very idea made him almost physically ill, so he gave up racing for good and went into coaching.

What do we make of these examples? Do they suggest that in some situations ultrarealism is useless? Not at all. Even when a successful comeback is impossible, it remains possible for the ultrarealist to make the best of the situation in other ways. But don't take it from me. Take it from Gabe Grunewald, the American runner who lost her life to cancer at 32. In one of her last interviews, when invited to contemplate her legacy, Gabe told *Runner's World*, "I hope what people mainly see is that you can still make something beautiful and something powerful out of a really bad situation. You can still find some good in it. I will never let cancer have the last word."

Even as she spoke these words, Gabe was in a situation she could not change. A comeback of any kind was completely out of the question. Nevertheless, Gabe recognized that she still possessed a certain freedom. She could still live bravely and joyfully and in doing so set a positive example for others instead of giving in to self-pity and bitterness. She could make the best of a seemingly hopeless situation by giving it a meaning she chose.

Remember, ultrarealism involves not wishing things were different than they are, no matter how bad they are. Of course Gabe did not want to die with so much living left undone, but by refusing to waste her time and energy on actively wishing that she didn't have cancer, she made the last part of her short life materially better than it would have been otherwise.

For the ultrarealist, the inability to consummate a comeback does not constitute failure, it merely shifts the terms of success. That's because, for the ultrarealist, success is not a particular result but the very *act* of making the best of a situation. Perhaps this is what Eliud Kipchoge was getting at when he said in his 2017 speech to the Oxford Union Society, "To win is not important. To be successful is not even important." Now, if you are Eliud Kipchoge, and you're preternaturally talented, and you never get injured, and you set a goal to become the first human to run a marathon in less than two hours, making the best of your situation might entail actually running a marathon in less than two hours, as he did in his second attempt. But if you're Gabe Grunewald, and you have cancer, and you set a goal to beat cancer and make the 2020 US Olympic Team, making the best of the situation might be setting an example to your fans and admirers before you pass away. In either case, you have been successful.

It's important not to confuse this capacity to turn failure into success with the sour grapes phenomenon described in Chapter 3. Sour grapes is about lying to yourself by pretending you never wanted something you are unable to get. Turning failure into success is not that at all. It is, rather, a matter of reaching for the next best alternative to those unattainable grapes.

There is no greater teacher on this subject than Viktor Frankl, an Austrian neurologist who spent four years in Nazi concentration camps during World War II. Of all the bad situations a human being might find himself in, few could be worse than the degradation, torture, sleeplessness, forced labor, starvation, and disease that Frankl and his fellow prisoners endured, yet even in this context, as Frankl reported in his memoir of the experience, *Man's Search for Meaning*, a select few found a kind of success in controlling what little they could. Frankl himself did so by looking out for his co-sufferers, standing up to their tormenters when he could, and continuing to practice his former profession, even developing the theory of logotherapy in his head while laying railroad tracks at night in frigid temperatures, shoeless. Frankl focused his psychologist's eye on ultrarealists he encountered in these awful places, writing that "the way they bore their suffering was a genuine inner achievement," which proved that "any man can, even under such circumstances, decide what shall become of him—mentally and spiritually."

I'm sure you didn't pick up this book expecting to be reminded of the horrors of the Holocaust, but I bring it up for a reason. The individuals who cope most successfully with the worst situations any human being can possibly go through are also the individuals who cope most successfully with the everyday challenges in life, including the challenges that athletes encounter in pursuit of their goals. Understanding how the men and women Frankl wrote about "bore their suffering" will help you bear yours, no matter how much smaller yours may seem in comparison. So, how *did* the heroes of the concentration camps bear their suffering? In two ways: by accepting the reality of their free will and by using this freedom to find meaning in their ordeal.

Philosopher Jean-Paul Sartre argued that the reality we fear more than any other is our own free will, for in acknowledging the freedom we have to make a choice of some kind in every situation, we accept responsibility for what becomes of us, at least inwardly. We all begin life as helpless infants, cared for by adults, and even after we become adults ourselves, a part of us still wants to be taken care of in some way—by fate, or God, or whatever; to *not* take responsibility for what becomes of us and yet still somehow always get what we want. Sartre's term for denying our freedom is *living in bad faith*, and it's something all of us do to one degree or another.

Well, almost all of us. Folks like Viktor Frankl offer proof that it is possible to live in complete good faith even when normal freedoms are denied us. But there are also other folks—perhaps more relatable to most of us—who show us what is gained when we learn to accept our free will in greater measure. Remember Evan from Chapter 1, the runner whom I helped to overcome a tendency to push too hard in training, and who, by learning how to be more real with himself, discovered a newfound feeling of control during the hardest moments of a race? This feeling is the reward that comes with accepting the reality of our freedom. Whereas nothing is scarier than taking full responsibility for what becomes of us before we do it, nothing feels better once we have done it because in owning our freedom, we gain the comfort of knowing we are in control, not of everything, but of the ultimate thing.

How interesting it is that the attitude that ultrarealists choose to adopt in situations where their attitude is the only thing they can control is one of finding meaning in their suffering. Frankl believed that meaning is the most fundamental human need. Even when basic physical needs are unsatisfied—when a person is malnourished, diseased, sleep-deprived, and in constant pain—they can still maintain the will to live if they feel their life has meaning. Recent psychology research offers support for this view, and indicates as well that the attitude ultrarealists choose to adopt in the most desperate situations is optimal—that finding meaning in experience makes people feel better and allows them to cope better than they would otherwise.

In a 2018 review, Colorado State University psychologist Michael Steger wrote, "Among the relationships that have been found repeatedly in the literature are positive correlations between meaning and happiness, life satisfaction, positive emotions, hope, self-esteem, autonomy, positive relationships with others, competence, extraversion, conscientiousness, health, and longevity . . . The body of evidence regarding meaning is large and growing quickly, and appears to reliably demonstrate the importance of meaning to human well-being and flourishing."

I've offered a lot of guidance in this book. Let me now offer one last bit, and if it's the only bit you remember and practice ten years from now, I won't be disappointed:

1) Accept the reality that you are free and can make some kind of choice in every situation, without exception.

2) Make the choice that makes your present situation most meaningful to you, not just in the worst situations, where your attitude is the only thing you can control, but in every situation, including those that are almost perfect but could be made just a little more perfect.

WHAT IS THE MEANING OF THIS?

Thirteen years, five months, and four days after Saul Raisin suffered the traumatic brain injury that changed the course of his life, we reconnected by telephone. His voice sounded exactly as it had when we'd first spoken 11 years before, a reminder that even after all this time he was still a young man—only 36, younger than some still-active pro cyclists.

Saul's voice was not the only sound that caught my attention during the call. The other was a rhythmic background thumping.

"Are you running right now?" I asked.

"I am," Saul said. "I do a lot more running than riding these days. I have a mountain bike with a set of road tires, but the last two times I rode it I almost got hit by cars. People don't pay attention around here."

"Here" is Newnan, Georgia, a quiet exurb of Atlanta, where Saul shares a modest three-bedroom home with his wife, Lindsey, and their son, Isaac. We discussed how Saul got there and whether he had finally succeeded in accepting, embracing, and addressing his post-accident reality. In this regard, I found him to be more forthcoming than he had been in 2008, when he was trying to project an image of inner peace and optimism—and perhaps also trying to convince himself he was doing okay. The need Saul felt then to distract himself from his festering grief injected a kind of desperation into his strivings. He crisscrossed the globe giving motivational speeches at a rate of 50 to 60 per year; threw himself into his work as an advocate for traumatic brain injury (TBI) survivors, which included volunteering for the Veterans Administration (VA); and trained like a professional triathlete. But his inner suffering made the frenetic pace unsustainable, and over time Saul withdrew, quitting the VA, limiting his speaking engagements to one or two a year, and abandoning triathlon.

He bottomed out in 2010. At 27, Saul was again living with his parents, jobless, caught up in another bad relationship, and drinking heavily. "I was kind of in that *why me* phase," he told me. "I was depressed and making poor life decisions." That summer, Saul visited Turner Field to catch an Atlanta Braves game. Upon arriving, he went straight to a concession stand to buy a beer. Recognizing him, the server came out from behind the counter and wrapped Saul in a bear hug, thanking him profusely and calling him "my hero." The source of these effusions was an Iraq War veteran and a fellow TBI sufferer, one of the many Saul had given hope through his caring one-on-one attention and also through his story. Caught off guard, Saul broke down in tears, feeling like a fraud. *If I don't start practicing what I preach,* he thought, *I'm not going to go anywhere.* Saul did not buy a beer after all, and in fact quit drinking altogether.

"I stopped saying, 'Why me?' and started saying, 'Why *not* me?'" Saul told me as he continued to run. "Do you know the saying, 'Never follow a leader who doesn't limp?' That's how I see myself now. What happened to me allows me to touch people in a way I never could before. It took me years to appreciate that."

There's an older veteran with a traumatic brain injury who lives in Saul's neighborhood. Saul takes him on errands and performs other small acts of kindness that have a greater, if narrower, impact than did his past efforts to lobby Congress for more support for vets with TBIs. What's more, the one-on-one work he does now suits him better. He feels good doing it in a way he never felt when trying to be the face of the movement.

A year after the Turner Field encounter that set Saul on his present course, he was visiting the Pediatric Neurotrauma Lab at Children's Healthcare in Atlanta when he met a young woman he felt an immediate connection with. After conversing with Lindsey for several minutes, Saul asked what he jokingly describes as the best pickup line ever: "Do you have a brain injury?"

Sure enough, she did. When she was 15, Lindsey was involved in an automobile accident that left her comatose for nine months. Like Saul, she was not expected to survive, but she surprised doctors by making an almost complete recovery. Saul and Lindsey started dating and were married in September 2014. Within three months, Lindsey, whose pelvis was completely shattered in the accident, was pregnant, again surprising her doctors, who had told her she could forget about ever becoming a mother. Despite some complications, Isaac arrived on schedule and healthy.

As for work, Saul describes himself as semiretired. On a typical day, he wakes up early and heads to the gym to lift weights. Both he and Lindsey are substitute teachers. On days when Saul doesn't teach, he spends the morning with Isaac, and then, after lunch, he goes for a run and works on his many home improvement projects. He enjoys cooking and prepares a majority of the family's evening meals.

Saul gets a little extra excitement from his side gig as an extra in movies and television shows. In recent years, Georgia has become known as the Hollywood of the East, and at any given time there is at least one project being filmed in Newnan. In 2018, Saul and Lindsey were strolling hand in hand downtown when they stumbled upon a production site, and something about it triggered the puppy in Saul like a tossed Frisbee.

"Hey, honey," he said. "There's a costume truck. I'm going to see if I can get into this movie!"

A couple of crewmen were hanging around outside the truck. Saul approached and asked where he needed to go for costume and makeup.

"We've been waiting for you!" one of them said.

Saul would find out later that the extra they'd been waiting for had been waylaid by a fender bender. It was just like in the movies! Saul spent the next several nights playing the role of a bar patron in a scene of *Summer Nights*, a *Grease* prequel. He has since walked on to more than 100 films and shows.

"Any chance you'll start going for speaking parts?" I asked.

"Nah, I don't need all that," Saul said.

By this point in the conversation, Saul had returned home from his run and suggested we switch to FaceTime so I could meet "the little monster," whom he found at the kitchen table, engrossed in some game of make-believe involving brightly colored pieces of plastic.

"Can you tell Mr. Matt what Daddy used to do?" Saul prompted.

"Ride bikes!" Isaac said.

When professional cycling was taken away from Saul, his life lost much of its meaning, and he became unhappy. For many years, he sought to regain happiness through surrogates for cycling, triathlon being the most obvious example. But these efforts amounted to little more than a denial of reality, a hopeless attempt to keep living the life he had loved so much. Only when

Saul had all but given up on happiness did a better way reveal itself to him. The beer server at Turner Field did not consider Saul his hero because he was kind to him. What made Saul a hero to the man was that he had raced bikes, and then almost died, and then *almost* come back all the way, which is a lot further than many TBI survivors get. What's more, in calling Saul his hero, the beer server had given him something in return. For it was then that Saul began to see his cycling career could have ongoing meaning in his life just as it was, a fleeting moment of glory that ended painfully and yet, to many, heroically.

Isaac figures into this new meaning as well. It was plain to see that, even at age 4, he took pride in his father's past athletic feats. I have some sense of what it may be like for him to grow up with Saul as a father because he reminds me of myself. My own father was a US Navy special forces operator during the Vietnam War, and although those days were long past by the time I was old enough to understand his service, and although my father never boasted of it but merely answered the questions my brothers and I asked and shared the occasional anecdote, I loved growing up as the child of a hero, as I perceived him, and I suspect Isaac will too, as Saul surely knows. There's meaning in that.

Saul still misses racing bikes. "I miss the fact that I could dominate," he told me shortly before we signed off FaceTime. "When you have a good day on the bike, you feel untouchable. I miss that rush." What's different now, though, is that he's okay with missing it. That's ultrarealism in a nutshell. In sport and in life, reality always gets the first move, but the mind, if it so chooses, gets the last one, and if it's the right move—one that locates the small pocket of freedom that forever exists within reality's confines, no matter how tightly they press—the mind always wins. Indeed, for the ultra-realist, comebacks *never* fail.

ACKNOWLEDGMENTS

I wish to offer my deepest gratitude to the following individuals for their invaluable contributions to this book, ranging from help with spelling to moral support: Christina Bauer, Casey Blaine and the fabulous team at VeloPress, Buck Blankenship, Courtney Cardenas, Suzanna Cohen, Curtis Cramblett, Sarah Crouch, Nataki Fitzgerald, Sean Fitzgerald, Rodney Flowers, Mario Fraioli, Evan Hardcastle, Greg Hillson, Mike Holmes, Justin Lucke, Rob Krar, Ed Mageean, Mandy McDougall, Wade Meyer, Cory Nyamora, Saul Raisin, Bill Rodgers, Ben Rosario, Josh Sandeman, Molly Seidel, Meghan Taff, Paul Thomas, Ryan Whited, and Jamie Whitmore. Extra special thanks to my friend and longtime agent, Linda Konner, who is truly the best in the business.

REFERENCES

Preface

Flowers, Rodney. *Get Up! I Can't. I Will. I Did . . . Here's How!* Toronto: Hasmark, 2015.

Wash, Vincent. "Is Sport the Brain's Biggest Challenge?" *Current Biology* 24, no. 18 (September 2014): 859–860.

Chapter 1

Alfano, Peter. "Joan Benoit Is Back on Course After a Month of Detours." *New York Times* (May 20, 1984). https://www.nytimes.com/1984/05/20/sports/joan-benoit-is-back-on-course-after -a-month-of-detours.html.

Benoit, Joan, with Sally Baker. *Running Tide.* New York: Alfred A. Knopf, 1987.

Goyanes, Cristina. "Mirinda Carfrae's Seemingly Impossible Surge to Win." espnW.com (October 7, 2015). https://www.espn.com/espnw/athletes-life/story/_/id/13829599/mirinda-carfrae-seemingly -impossible-surge-win.

Chapter 2

Dennehy, Cathal. "Despite Insoles Coming Loose, Eliud Kipchoge Wins Berlin Marathon." *Runner's World* (September 27, 2015).

Emerson, Ralph Waldo. *Self-Reliance and Other Essays.* Seattle: AmazonClassics, 2017.

Epictetus. *The Art of Living: The Classical Manual on Virtue, Happiness, and Effectiveness.* New York: HarperOne, 2013.

Glasser, William. *Positive Addiction.* New York: Harper Colophon, 1985.

Glasser, William. *Reality Therapy: A New Approach to Psychiatry.* New York: Harper & Row, 1965.

Ivanova, Elena, Dennis Jensen, Jamie Cassoff, Fei Gu, and Bärbel Knäuper. "Acceptance and Commitment Therapy Improves Exercise Tolerance in Sedentary Women." *Medicine & Science in Sports & Exercise* 47, no. 6 (June 2015): 1251–1258.

Kabat-Zinn, Jon. *Full Catastrophe Living: Using the Wisdom of Your Body and Mind to Face Stress, Pain, and Illness.* New York: Bantam, 1990.

Laërtius, Diogenes. *Lives and Opinions of Eminent Philosophers.* Chicago: e-artnow, 2020.

Raviv, Shaun. "The Genius Neuroscientist Who Might Hold the Key to True AI." Wired.com (November 13, 2018). https://www.wired.com/story/karl-friston-free-energy-principle-artificial intelligence/#:~:text=Karl%20Friston's%20free%20energy%20principle,the%20mind%20of%20 Friston%20himself.

Sims, Graem. *Why Die? The Extraordinary Percy Cerutty, "Maker of Champions."* Seattle: Amazon, 2020.

Chapter 3

Aesop. *The Complete Fables.* New York: Penguin, 2003.

Chung, Misook Lee, Terry Lennie, and Debra Moser. "Adherence to a Low-Sodium Diet in Patients with Heart Failure Is Best When Family Members Also Follow the Diet: A Multicenter Observational Study." *Journal of Cardiovascular Nursing* 30, no. 1 (January–February 2015): 44–50. https://doi.org/10.1097/JCN.0000000000000089.

Fitzgerald, Matt. *Life Is a Marathon: A Memoir of Love and Endurance.* Berkeley: Da Capo Lifelong, 2019.

Hansen, Ernst Albin, Anders Emanuelsen, Robert Mørkegaard Gertsen, and S. R. Sørensen. "Improved Marathon Performance by Improved In-Race Nutritional Strategy Intervention." *International Journal of Sport Nutrition and Exercise Metabolism* 24, no. 6: 645–655. https://doi.org/10.1123/ijsnem.2013-0130.

Hutchinson, Alex. "To Eat on the Go, Endurance Athletes Need to Train Their Stomachs." *The Globe and Mail* (April 19, 2017). https://www.theglobeandmail.com/life/health-and-fitness/health/to-eat-on-the-go-endurance-athletes-need-to-train-their-stomachs/article34748787/.

Janoff-Bulman, Ronnie. *Shattered Assumptions: Towards a New Psychology of Trauma.* New York: Free Press, 1992.

Olympic Channel. "The Most Incredible Determination in the Olympics" (Petra Majdič). *Against All Odds* Season 1, Episode 8 (2016). YouTube video, 25:35. https://www.youtube.com/watch?v=D-FInpfcb8b0.

Rodgers, Bill. "Bill Rodgers' 1974 Training Log." (1974). https://static1.squarespace.com/static/5563d3dee4b00576f8432210/t/5b76e7591ae6cf7124f3c320/1534519130650/35802948-billRodgers1974LOG.pdf.

Shermer, Michael. *The Believing Brain.* New York: Griffin, 2012.

Chapter 4

Anderson, C. R. "Locus of Control, Coping Behaviors, and Performance in a Stress Setting: A Longitudinal Study." *Journal of Applied Psychology* 62, no. 4 (1977): 446–451. http://doi.org/10.1037/0021-9010.62.4.446.

Cleese, John, Terry Jones, and Terry Gilliam. *Monty Python and the Holy Grail.* EMI Films, 1975.

Dweck, Carol. *Mindset: The New Psychology of Success.* New York: Ballantine, 2007.

Fraioli, Mario. "Gabe and Justin Grunewald." *The Morning Shakeout* (October 2, 2018). Podcast. https://themorningshakeout.com/podcast-episode-31-with-gabe-and-justin-grunewald/.

Frias, Araceli, Philip Watkins, Amy Webber, and Jeffrey Froh. "Death and Gratitude: Death Reflection Enhances Gratitude." *The Journal of Positive Psychology* 6, no. 2 (March 2011): 154–162. http://doi.org/10.1080/17439760.2011.558848.

Robb, Sharon. "Laursen Wins Another Despite Borrowed Gear, Sore Tendon." *South Florida Sun Sentinel* (June 28, 1999). https://www.sun-sentinel.com/news/fl-xpm-1999-06-28-9906280118-story.html.

Stone, Mark, Kevin Thomas, Michael Wilkinson, Emma Stevenson, Alan St. Clair Gibson, Andrew Jones, and Kevin Thompson. "Exploring the Performance Reserve: Effect of Different Magnitudes of Power Output Deception on 4,000 m Cycling Time-Trial Performance." *PLoS One* (March 9, 2017). http://doi.org/10.1371/journal.pone.0173120.

Studio Soresi. "Depressions: A Few Moments from 30 Miles in the Canyon" (Rob Krar). YouTube video, 7:39. (December 14, 2014). https://www.youtube.com/watch?v=zSQUXTiTaoM.

Tedeschi, Richard, and Lawrence Calhoun. *Trauma and Transformation: Growth in the Aftermath of Suffering*. Berkeley: SAGE Publications, 1995.

Tilney McDonough, Victoria. "The Many Layers of Post-Traumatic Growth." BrainLine (May 23, 2012).

Van Dernoot Lipsky, Laura, and Connie Burk. *Trauma Stewardship*. Oakland: Berrett-Koehler Publishers, 2009.

Yang, Billy. "Rob Krar." *Billy Yang Podcast* (August 18, 2018). Podcast. https://billyyangpodcast.libsyn.com/rob-krar-byp-020.

Chapter 5

Badwater AdventureCORPS. "2007 Badwater: David Goggins Finishes" (Post-race interview with Badwater Ultramarathon Race Director Chris Kostman). YouTube video, 7:33 (July 25, 2007). https://www.youtube.com/watch?v=EH08BpU9XCw.

Corrion, Karine, Valérie Morales, Alessandro Bergamaschi, Bernard Massiera, Jean-Benoit Morin, and Fabienne d'Arippe-Longueville. "Psychosocial Factors as Predictors of Dropout in Ultra-Trailers." *PLoS One* (November 5, 2018). https://doi.org/10.1371/journal.pone.0206498.

Farrelly, Peter, dir. *Dumb and Dumber*. (Starring Jim Carrey). New Line Cinema, 1994.

Fitzgerald, Matt. "Why Run Streaking Isn't as Insane as It Sounds." Podiumrunner.com (June 3, 2019). https://www.podiumrunner.com/training/why-run-streaking-isnt-as-insane-as-it-sounds/.

Goggins, David, and Adam Skolnick. *Can't Hurt Me: Master Your Mind and Defy the Odds*. Austin: Scribe Media, 2018.

Gourley, Jim. "The Toughest Man Alive." *Triathlete* (August 2009).

Samuele Marcora. "Do We Really Need a Central Governor to Explain Brain Regulation of Exercise Performance?" *European Journal of Applied Physiology* 104 (2008): 929–931.

Sang, Patrick. "Patrick Sang on Eliud Kipchoge." INEOS 1:59 Challenge website (July 12, 2019). https://www.ineos159challenge.com/news/patrick-sang-on-eliud-kipchoge/.

Wilson, Chris, and Brett Witter. *The Master Plan: My Journey from Life in Prison to a Life of Purpose*. New York: J. P. Putnam's Sons, 2019.

Chapter 6

Carlson, Timothy. "Jamie's Choice: Risk for Freedom." Slowtwitch.com (June 16, 2009). https://www.slowtwitch.com/Features/Jamie_s_Choice_Risk_for_freedom__866.html.

———. "Jamie Whitmore: A New Life." Slowtwitch.com (June 23, 2009). https://www.slowtwitch.com/Features/Jamie_Whitmore_A_New_Life_879.html.

———. "Jamie Whitmore Battles Cancer." Slowtwitch.com (June 15, 2009). https://www.slowtwitch.com/Features/Jamie_Whitmore_fights_cancer_863.html.

———. "Jamie Whitmore's Greatest Victory." Slowtwitch.com (June 12, 2009). https://www.slowtwitch.com/Features/Jamie_Whitmore_s_greatest_victory__855.htm.

XTERRA TV. "2002 XTERRA World Championship." Vimeo video, 44:11. (June 29, 2015). https://vimeo.com/channels/xterra20/132172899.

———. "2004 XTERRA World Championship." Vimeo video, 52:04 (July 13, 2015). https://vimeo.com/channels/xterra20/133374546.

Chapter 7

Barnicle, Scott. "Enjoyment, Mental Skills Training, and Performance Enhancement in Elite Women's Soccer: A Case Study Example." *Journal of Performance Psychology* 10 (2017): 1–15.

Cho, Cecile, and Theresa Cho. "On Averting Negative Emotion: Remedying the Impact of Shifting Expectations." *Frontiers in Psychology* (November 20, 2018). https://doi.org/10.3389/fpsyg.2018.02121.

Ede, Alison, Philip Sullivan, and Deborah Feltz. "Self-Doubt: Uncertainty as a Motivation Factor on Effort in an Exercise Endurance Task." *Psychology of Sport and Exercise* 28 (2017): 31–34. https://doi.org/10.1016/j.psychsport.2016.10.002.

FloTrack. "800m Runner-Up Ajeé Wilson Says Caster Semenya Should Be Allowed to Compete." YouTube video, 1:37 (June 30, 2019). https://www.youtube.com/watch?v=V2aCwTiP-qM.

Grainger, Katherine. *Dreams Do Come True*. London: Andre Deutsch, 2013.

Halvorson, Gary, dir., David Crane, Marta Kauffman, Sherry Bilsing, and Ellen Kreamer. "The One Where Phoebe Runs." *Friends*. Season 6, Episode 7. NBC. (November 11, 1999).

Olympic Channel. "Katherine Grainger Relives Her Olympic Journey." YouTube video, 9:19 (August 30, 2015). https://www.youtube.com/watch?v=mdNzefoyxZ4&t=313s.

Olympic Channel. "Olympic Champion Katherine Grainger Returns to Rowing—Road to Rio 2016." YouTube video, 5:35 (October 27, 2014). https://www.youtube.com/watch?v=qrFbBOVS-8E.

McBean, Marnie. "Your Want-To Sweet Spot." Marnie McBean (blog) (June 1, 2012). http://marniemcbean.ca/your-want-to-sweet-spot/.

TheBeanyman. "Katherine Grainger & Vicky Thornley Interview on Winning Silver in Double Sculls—Rio Olympics. YouTube video, 6:14 (August 21, 2016). https://www.youtube.com/watch?v=XD1_fVgEfcg.

Wilson, Kylie, and Darren Brookfield. "Effect of Goal Setting on Motivation and Adherence in a Six-Week Exercise Program." *International Journal of Sport and Exercise Psychology* 7, no. 1 (2009): 89–100. https://doi.org/10.1080/1612197X.2009.9671894.

REFERENCES

Chapter 8

Arthur, Bruce. "Sink or Swim: How the Ironman Saved Lionel Sanders from Himself." *The Star.* (September 19, 2015). https://www.thestar.com/sports/2015/09/19/sink-or-swim-how-the-ironman-saved-lionel-sanders-from-himself.html.

Axon, Rachel. "World-Class Triathlete Lionel Sanders Battled Drug Addiction." *USA Today* (June 30, 2015). https://www.usatoday.com/story/sports/olympics/2015/06/30/lionel-sanders-triathlon-ironman-world-championships/29523097/.

Culp, Brad. "How Lionel Sanders Became Every Triathlete's Hero." Triathlete.com (October 4, 2018). https://www.triathlete.com/culture/people/how-lionel-sanders-became-every-triathletes-hero/.

Duff, Bob. "Harrow's Lionel Sanders Answers Ironman Challenge." *The Vancouver Sun* (October 12, 2015). http://www.vancouversun.com/Duff+Harrow+Lionel+Sanders+answers+Ironman+challenge/11432301/story.html.

Giordano, Dana. "More Than Running: Molly Seidel, 2020 US Olympic Marathon Trials Runner-Up, Pro Runner for Saucony." *More Than Running* (April 27, 2020). Podcast. http://citiusmag.com/podcast/more-than-running-podcast-molly-seidel/.

Hanlon, Julia. "Molly Seidel on Navigating Mental Health and Running Professionally." *Running on Om* (January 14, 2020). Podcast. https://www.listennotes.com/podcasts/running-on-om/225-molly-seidel-on-NfbxutIHThO/.

Maslow, Abraham. *The Farther Reaches of Human Nature.* New York: Viking, 1973.

Nietzsche, Friedrich. *The Gay Science.* New York: Vintage, 1974.

Sanders, Lionel. Lionel Sanders (website). https://www.lsanderstri.com.

Uzielli, Julian. "Six Years Ago, Lionel Sanders Was a Drug Addict. Now He's a Top Ironman Athlete." *The Globe and Mail* (September 27, 2015). https://www.theglobeandmail.com/life/health-and-fitness/fitness/you-can-create-your-own-limits/article26540153/.

Chapter 9

Ator, Jen. "Kara Goucher Is Changing Course." *Women's Running* (November 15, 2019). https://www.womensrunning.com/culture/people/kara-goucher-changing-course/.

Fitzgerald, Matt. "Iron Heart." *Triathlete* (April 2004).

Fitzgerald, Matt. "More Than a Comeback." *Triathlete* (January 2009).

Frankl, Viktor. *Man's Search for Meaning.* Boston: Beacon Press, 1967.

Palermo, Pablo Martin. "Interview: Saul Raisin." Ciclismo International (2013). https://www.ciclismointernacional.com/interviewsaul-raisin/.

Raisin, Saul, with Dave Shields. *Tour de Life: My Journey from Coma to Competition.* Salt Lake City: Three Story Press, 2011.

Steger, Michael. "Meaning and Well-Being." *Handbook of Well-Being.* Salt Lake City: DEF Publishers, 2018.

Strout, Erin. "Gabrielle 'Gabe' Grunewald Refused to Let Cancer Have the Last Word." *Runner's World* (June 12, 2009). https://www.runnersworld.com/runners-stories/a27469714/gabriele-grunewald-american-runner/.

Yount, Michael. "Cyclist Beats Odds after Brain Injury." *Salt Lake City Tribune* (July 8, 2001). https://archive.sltrib.com/story.php?ref=/sports/ci_6325448.

INDEX

INDEX

ABOUT THE AUTHOR

Matt Fitzgerald is a highly acclaimed endurance sports author, coach, and nutritionist. His many books include *How Bad Do You Want It?*, *Racing Weight*, and *Run: The Mind-Body Method of Running by Feel*. Matt's writing has also appeared in numerous magazines, including *Outside* and *Runner's World*, and on popular websites such as podium-runner.com and nbcnews.com. He is a cofounder and co-head coach of 80/20 Endurance and the creator of the Diet Quality Score smartphone app. A lifelong endurance athlete, he speaks frequently at events throughout the United States and internationally.